5 BIG IDEAS

for Cradle Catholics

FOR THOSE WHO'VE LEFT THE CHURCH
OR JUST AREN'T GROWING

FIND THE PEACE THAT YOU'VE WISHED
OTHERS AT EVERY MASS

Patrick J. McGarrity

Collaborators:

Mom, Melissa, John W., Mark, Carla, Paul, Cyndi, Jeff S., Joe, Mary A., Ev.

5 BIG IDEAS

for Cradle Catholics

FOR THOSE WHO'VE LEFT THE CHURCH
OR JUST AREN'T GROWING

FIND THE PEACE YOU'VE WISHED
OTHERS AT EVERY MASS

A FREE PDF OF THE BOOK MAY BE DOWNLOADED FROM THE FOLLOWING SITE:
www.clairtonenterprises.com/5BigIdeas

CONTENTS

"Peace Be With You"

As a Cradle Catholic you've wished others "peace"
hundreds or even thousands of times as part of the weekly Mass. . .
. . .everyone sitting around you, every time you went to Mass

The purpose of this book is to help you *actually experience* that peace. . .
to help you experience what *you have wished others* at every Mass
even though *you* haven't experienced that deep sense of peace yourself, not yet
whether you've left the Catholic Church or are still in it,
if you were born into the Catholic Church, this book is for you

may peace be with *you*

What's a Big Idea?

A "Big Idea" generally means a concept or idea
that can have a dramatic, positive impact
on a person or on an organization
if understood and put into practice

I grew up in the Catholic Church. I'm a "Cradle Catholic". Almost every week of the first eighteen years of my life I went to Mass on Sunday (or Saturday). At various times later in life I either went to Mass every week, went to Mass once in a while, or didn't go to Mass at all. At every Mass I shook hands with or kissed those around me and said to them, "peace be with you" or simply "peace."

Only within the past few years of my life (I'm 48) have I understood what that peace actually means. The only way to really understand the meaning of that peace, the peace Catholics wish each other at every Mass, the peace that Jesus spoke about and taught about, the peace that Paul and Peter wrote about after Jesus left, the peace that Isaiah wrote about Jesus bringing 700 years *before* Jesus was born, the peace that Jerusalem ("the city of peace") is named after, the peace that Jews wish others in greeting and departing ("Shalom"), the peace that Arabs wish others in greeting and departing ("Salaám al"), is to experience it yourself. You'll know it when you get there.

For most of my life I wasn't experiencing a deep sense of peace, maybe you can relate to some of these ways of "living" that are anything but peaceful:

- I regularly expressed anger; I worried a lot about the future; I was anxious

- Most of my decisions were based on some combination of fear, greed, impatience or lust

- I was very focused on serving myself and my needs; when hurt or offended by others I sought payback

- I wasn't faithful in relationships, I cycled through multiple relationships quickly

- I didn't respect the bond of marriage of others. I had many, many sexual relationships with women that didn't result in a life-long relationship

- I was so focused on work and investments that I lived a life completely out of balance, a life that wasn't sustainable

- At times in my life I drank a lot, seeming to test the outer bounds of how much alcohol the body can process

- While hospitalized, I was diagnosed as bi-polar, schizophrenic, or the exceedingly vague: "Psychosis NOS". The "NOS" means "Not Otherwise Specified"

I was nowhere near a deep sense of peace. The tangible results of my ways of "living" are telling: a night in jail, three divorces (one mine, plus two other couples), two weeks in the mental health ward of a hospital, and scores of broken relationships.

Once I hit bottom, I tried the usual things that people try: anti-psychotic drugs, a psychiatrist, a couple different therapists, alcohol. I was working the problem from the wrong side. I was trying to fix myself through a variety of modern techniques when what I really needed was a complete transformation of myself. Once you're given a mental health diagnosis, the world considers you broken to the point of never overcoming your brokenness. I think that's why everyone keeps mental health histories secret. The 5 BIG IDEAS point to another path. A path laid out by "The Great Physician", Jesus.

Any Masses I did attend in the first forty or so years of my life, I said to those around me at Mass, "peace be with you" or just "peace," having no idea what those words really meant, having no idea what it felt like to experience such a peace.

I now know what those words mean. I now know what it feels like to experience a deep sense of peace. I eventually found a deep sense of peace through a process of understanding, insight, and specific actions that I have come to call the "5 BIG IDEAS for Cradle Catholics." The process took me about five years to work through.

I believe you can make your way through the 5 BIG IDEAS much faster than I did and achieve the same result, making use of this guidebook, the plans within it that you can adjust, and the resources mentioned. On your own or through a study group, you can probably make your way through the 5 BIG IDEAS in a few months, maybe a year, finding a deep sense of peace and a joy for life. Then again, it may take you longer than five years. The amount of time elapsed doesn't matter. What matters is that you find that deep sense of peace and joy for life.

I don't believe the 5 BIG IDEAS are limited to those who have a mental health history, but to all Cradle Catholics. If you grew up in the Catholic Church you're a Cradle Catholic too, regardless of your current relationship with the Catholic Church. You likely fall into one of these categories, or bounced around more than one over time like I have:

- You've left the Catholic Church and just don't participate in any organized religion

- You're looking for an alternate form of Christianity from Catholicism but haven't quite found what you're looking for yet, and are actively searching

- You've found another Christian denomination or non-denominational Christian church

- You're a "member" of the Catholic Church but don't participate at all

- You're a "member" of the Catholic Church but go to Mass infrequently

Regardless of your current relationship with organized religion of any type, you're still a Cradle Catholic if you grew up in the Catholic Church. You can't undo the years of participation you've had in the Catholic Church, nor should you want to, there's value in your experience. The 5 BIG IDEAS help you tap into that experience and grow. I believe that all Cradle Catholics are prepared to find the deep sense of peace that I've found.

Many people *do* find a deep sense of peace in the Catholic Church, but a disturbingly high proportion of

Cradle Catholics do not. This book is not for the former group of people, but for the latter. The path I've found to the peace that Catholics wish each other at every Mass every weekend can be found by many, many others, whether they're still in the Catholic Church or not.

That's the purpose of this book, to help you take advantage of your preparation as a Cradle Catholic to transform your life and find a deep sense of peace you've only wished for others, not experienced yourself, not yet.

I've read books written by Bishops and some very nice, probably very righteous Catholics that are intended to help you become more "Catholic". This book is different. It's written by a sinner who's screwed up a lot, who's made a lot of mistakes, but over the course of about five years has stumbled upon a path that transformed him. I believe the 5 BIG IDEAS and the resulting transformation are repeatable. You too can experience a deep sense of peace you've never known but wished upon others at every Mass you've ever attended. You'll need to do some work. Don't just glance at the plans for each BIG IDEA, work through them and complete them.

Peace be with *you*.

Patrick J. McGarrity
September, 2015

Why this Book?

"And this is the will of him who sent me,

that I shall lose none of all those he has given me,

but raise them up at the last day."

"For my Father's will is that everyone

who looks to the Son and believes in him shall have eternal life,

and I will raise them up at the last day."

– Jesus in the Gospel of John, 6: 39-40

> ℘Cℜ
> ## Ask yourself this one simple question:
> ## Are you at peace right now?
> ℘Cℜ

INTRO: Why this Book?

777,423 children were baptized into the Catholic Church in 2013 in the United States, *13.7 million* children worldwide[1]

How many of the 13.7 million children baptized into the Catholic Church each year ever get to the point of experiencing the peace that Catholics wish each other at every Mass every week?

Forget about your season of life. Forget about where you are in your spiritual journey. Forget about your relationship with the Catholic Church or any other organized religion. Forget about your relationship with your family or your spouse or your Mom or your Dad or whoever is the most Catholic person you know. Ask yourself this one simple question: Are you at peace right now? Do you have this deep sense of peace that you wished everyone around you at every Mass you ever attended?

> ℘Cℜ
> ## A deep dense of peace. It's difficult to
> ## pin down what that is, but I'll try...
> ℘Cℜ

A deep sense of peace. It's difficult to pin down what that is, but I'll try. A deep sense of peace is...

- a sense that you're where you should be right now, doing what you should be doing, even if you'll be somewhere else later doing something different.

- a sense that nothing anyone does to you or says to you can affect you. Maybe you're affected for a short while, but then the affect on you quickly fades, as you return to a deep sense of peace.

- a different sense of time than you had previously. Your sense of time is different than most people around you. Waiting in line is an opportunity to meet people or reflect, not a cause for anger or inconvenience. Things seem to have a natural pace which you honor, not try to compress.

- a recognition that many people you encounter or observe in your daily life don't have a deep sense of peace. Based on what they do or what they say when you're with them or just near them, you know they don't share your deep sense of peace. You wish they did.

If you were born and raised in the Catholic Church and don't live life with a deep sense of peace, if you

---

1 accessed from cara.georgetown.edu/CARAServices/requestedchurchstats.html on September 8, 2014 and July 17, 2015. Statistics are the most recent years available. Number represents the number of infants (713,302) and other minors (64,121) Baptized into the Catholic Church in the United States of America in 2013. In comparison, 38,042 adults were baptized into the Catholic Church in the USA in the same year, so of the 815,465 people who entered the Catholic Church, about 5% were adults and 95% were minors, with 87% of all baptisms being infant baptisms. The worldwide number is from the same website.

don't have a joy and appreciation for life, this book is for you. The 5 BIG IDEAS lay down a path to peace that you can follow.

If you're a Cradle Catholic and you don't feel a deep sense of peace, you're not alone. According to a recent survey by the Pew Charitable Trust, of the approximately 245 million adults in America, 78 million were raised Catholic[2]. So, about one-third of all adults in America are Cradle Catholic, one-third of every adult in America was born and raised in the Catholic Church. That's a surprisingly large proportion of the overall population of people in the United States, even for someone like me, who grew up surrounded by Catholics.

> ഐൻ൪
> ## About one-third of all adults in America are Cradle Catholic
> ഐൻ൪

As a tutor, I'm amazed by how many of the students or parents of students I work with are Cradle Catholics. In the process of writing this book, I was surprised to find out my eye doctor grew up in the Catholic church. After I received the first proof of this book back from the printer I was reviewing it in a Chick-fil-A restaurant. Two of the employees asked what I was doing. It turns out that they each have family members that might find this book useful.

While I've been aware of the Catholic statistics for a while, I didn't really understand the practical meaning of the statistics. Now, I assume that everyone I meet either grew up in the Catholic Church or knows someone close to them that did, and that assumption typically turns out to be true. If I have truly stumbled upon something significant, every person I meet could benefit personally from the 5 BIG IDEAS or knows someone close to

> ഐൻ൪
> ## Now, I assume everyone I meet either grew up in the Catholic Church or knows someone close to them that did.
> ഐൻ൪

them that could. Whether you're still in the Catholic Church or not has no impact on your being a Cradle Catholic. All Cradle Catholics share a core common understanding and common experience. The point of this book is to make use of that core common understanding and experience, make a few adjustments or additions, and achieve an incredible result: help you find your way to a deep sense of peace you've only wished for others, not experienced yourself.

One indication that many Cradle Catholics aren't experiencing a deep sense of peace is that many have left the church. Forty-one percent of Cradle Catholics in America have left the Catholic Church as of 2014, up from about 33% in 2011[3]. Just the people that have left the church, if they were a church, would be the

---

2 Statistics from www.pewforum.org/2015/05/12/americas-changing-religious-landscape/ page 6 of 16.
3 "The Hidden Exodus: Catholics becoming Protestants", by Thomas Reese, National Catholic Reporter, April, 18, 2011 is the source of the 2011 statistic, and the Pew Research Center's update of its Religious Landscape

second largest church in America, behind the Catholic Church, but larger than other Christian denominations such as the Methodist or Lutheran denominations, and ahead of the Evangelical churches. That's a surprisingly large group of people.

While many Cradle Catholics have left the Church, about half of those who have left haven't joined another faith community. Pollsters have developed a category for anyone who isn't currently affiliated with a congregation of any type, they fit into a category called "nones", which means they have no affiliation with any church. Cradle Catholic "nones" are a large group, about 1 of every 20 Americans, about 5% of every adult in America. We're definitely designed to grow, develop, worship and enjoy fellowship in groups. I don't believe that anyone who's left the Catholic Church and who hasn't become an active part of another faith community has found a deep sense of peace. I believe they're just stuck. They're stuck because they don't know what to do next. Are you stuck? I was.

> ℰℑℭℛ
>
> **All of these statistics are interesting but irrelevant. The only statistic that really matters is you.**
>
> ℰℑℭℛ

Many Cradle Catholics remain in the Catholic Church but aren't especially active in the Church. I'm fairly certain that they aren't experiencing a deep sense of peace, even if they wish others peace at every Mass they attend. The Pew Charitable Trust's surveys of religious practices and beliefs in the United States[4] point to many in the Catholic Church who are Catholic by birth and still identify themselves as Catholic, but aren't active in the Church. Of those in the survey who identify themselves as Catholic:

> **42% attend Mass once a week or more**, these are the "active" Catholics, most of the people you would see at a Mass.

> **39% attend Mass from a few times a year to as often as once or twice a month.** I suspect these Cradle Catholics are going to Mass out of habit or some sense of obligation. Most could be considered "non practicing" Catholics.

> **19% attend Mass seldom or never**, clearly "non practicing" Catholics.

The highly varying levels of participation in worship through the Mass may be a rough indication of the highly varying levels of people who experience a deep sense of peace of the Catholics who remain affiliated with the Catholic Church. It's difficult to imagine a Cradle Catholic growing up in the Catholic

---

Survey is the source of the 2014 statistic (www.pewforum.org/2015/05/12/americas-changing-religious-landscape/.

4   Accessed from http://religions.pewforum.org/portraits on November 6, 2014. Detailed results: 9% attend Mass more than once per week, 33% once per week, 19% once or twice a month, 20% a few times a year, 13% seldom, and 6% never.

Church, choosing to stay in the Church, experiencing a deep sense of peace, and not being an active member of their parish. Going to Mass once each week would be a minimum level of participation. I would expect they would be doing much, much more than just attending weekly Mass: they would be volunteering, teaching, encouraging others, serving others, etc.

All of these statistics are interesting but irrelevant. The only statistic that matters is you. Either you're experiencing a deep sense of peace or you're not. It's a binary question, like a light switch: off or on, yes or no. There is no "sort of". If you are, you'll know it. If you're unsure, then you're not.

If you are experiencing a deep sense of peace, give this book to someone else. If you're not experiencing a deep sense of peace or you're uncertain whether you are or you aren't, read about each of the 5 BIG IDEAS and work through the simple plans provided to put each into practice.

The quotation at the start of this chapter is directly relevant to you. Your value to God cannot be measured, you are infinitely important. If you aren't experiencing a deep sense of peace, you're "lost" from God's point of view. Jesus told a story to his entourage of followers that is retold in the Gospel of Luke. The story describes how God feels about the "lost":

> ෨෬
> **"Rejoice with me;
> I have found my lost sheep"**
> ෨෬

Now the tax collectors and sinners were all gathering around to hear Jesus. But the Pharisees and the teachers of the law muttered, "This man welcomes sinners and eats with them." Then Jesus told them this parable:

"Suppose one of you has a hundred sheep and loses one of them. Doesn't he leave the ninety-nine in the open country and go after the lost sheep until he finds it? And when he finds it, he joyfully puts it on his shoulders and goes home. Then he calls his friends and neighbors together and says, 'Rejoice with me; I have found my lost sheep.'

"I tell you that in the same way there will be more rejoicing in heaven over one sinner who repents than over ninety-nine righteous persons who do not need to repent." (Gospel of Luke, Chapter 15, verses 1-7)

Jesus didn't come into the world for the people who have it all figured out. Jesus came into the world for sinners like you and like me. You and I are that one lost sheep. The 5 BIG IDEAS can help you be found. The 5 BIG IDEAS can help you find a deep sense of peace you've only wished for others. Let God find you, read and put into practice the 5 BIG IDEAS.

Where Do Cradle Catholics Go?[5]

Some Cradle Catholics remain active in a parish, some leave and find another Christian church community, some remain in the Church but are "not practicing", some leave the Church but don't go anywhere else. The chart below describes where Cradle Catholics go based on survey statistics.

For every 100 Cradle Catholics in America...	Number of Cradle Catholics
28 remain in the Catholic Church and attend Mass at least weekly	☺☺☺☺☺ ☺☺☺☺☺ ☺☺☺☺☺ ☺☺☺☺☺ ☺☺☺☺☺ ☺☺☺
17 have left the Catholic Church and are affiliated with another Christian denomination	☺☺☺☺☺ ☺☺☺☺☺ ☺☺☺☺☺ ☺☺
38 remain in the Catholic Church but attend mass less than weekly or not at all	☹☹☹☹☹ ☹☹☹☹☹ ☹☹☹☹☹ ☹☹☹☹☹ ☹☹☹☹☹ ☹☹☹☹☹ ☹☹☹☹☹ ☹☹☹
17 have left the Catholic Church and are not affiliated with any other church	☹☹☹☹☹ ☹☹☹☹☹ ☹☹☹☹☹ ☹☹

This book is mainly written for the 55% of Cradle Catholics who fall into the last two rows in the chart above. If that is you, this book is written for you.

If you fall into the second row in the chart above, you may benefit from this book, it depends on where you are in your journey. If you're in the group represented by the first row in the chart above, this book is probably not for you, give this book to someone else you know that falls within the last two rows.

I've experienced each of the four categories of Cradle Catholics listed above at one point in my life or another. Some of the categories I've been in more than once across different seasons of my life.

---

5   Chart based on data from the Pew Charitable Trust, with statistical analysis performed on the raw data. Any error is the author's.

Our Catholic Upbringing Prepares Us to Find Peace

I grew up in a large Irish Catholic family in New Jersey, where my entire extended family was Catholic and most of the people I knew were Catholic.

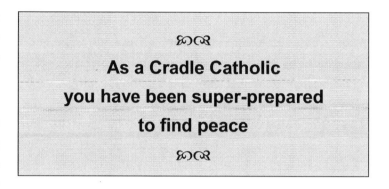

As a Cradle Catholic
you have been super-prepared
to find peace

I'm a "Cradle Catholic." That is, I've been Catholic since birth. If you were born into a Catholic family and raised Catholic, you too are a Cradle Catholic. I went to church every week with my family. I was an altar boy. I went to our Church's Elementary school for a few years[6] and attended a Catholic High School. My first marriage was in a Catholic Church.

In spite of that privileged start to life, I just didn't get it. I was surrounded and immersed in the Catholic Church, but I didn't understand the *basics* of what it means to be a Christian, a follower of Jesus, and I definitely didn't *act* like a follower of Jesus. I was nowhere near having a sense of peace. Because of my upbringing as a Cradle Catholic, though, I was well prepared to find a deep sense of peace later in life. In just the 18 years I lived with my family in New Jersey, I:

- **Listened to more than 179 hours of Bible readings** from the Old and New Testament as part of weekly and major holiday mass attendance[7]

- **Recited the Lord's Prayer more than 700 times** as part of weekly mass attendance[8]

- **Attended more than 300 hours of religious instruction** as part of "CCD", or Catholic Religious instruction on Sundays in elementary school and on Wednesday nights in High School[9]

- **Sung more than 2,800 hymns** as part of weekly mass attendance[10]

Of course, the level of participation in the Church varies widely across families. What has been your level of participation in the Catholic Church over the course of your life so far? How have you been prepared to find peace? Whatever level of participation, the 5 BIG IDEAS can move you forward.

---

6   My brother Mike's long-held opinion is that I wanted to go to the Catholic elementary school so that I could ride the bus to school rather than walk the 7/10 of a mile to the public school. Perhaps. Karen, my best friend who lived up the street, was planning to go there, that gave me the idea of going to the Catholic school, St. Catherine of Siena.

7   Assumptions: 15 minutes of Bible readings per week just counting the First Reading, Second Reading, Responsorial Psalm, and the Gospel reading; 55 masses attended per year, from age 5 through 18: $(15*55*13)/60 = 178.75$. This doesn't count the verses from the Bible that are embedded within the mass itself outside the formal Biblical readings at mass which would drive this number significantly higher, doubling or even tripling the total Biblical reading count of hours.

8   Assumptions: the Lord's Prayer (or Our Father) is recited at every mass, 55 masses attended per year, from age 5 through 18.

9   Assumptions: 13 years of religious instruction Sunday mornings or on Wednesday evenings through high school, 25 hours per year $(13*25 = 325)$

10 Assumptions: 13 years of 4 Hymns sung at each mass: Processional/Opening, Offertory, Communion, and Closing.

If you grew up in a Catholic family and had any involvement in the Church, you have been prepared to find a deep sense of peace. It really doesn't matter whether you're still active in a parish, have left the church and have found another faith community, or you've just stopped participating in any Christian group. The preparation has already been done, the seed has been sown.

While well prepared to find a deep sense of peace that Catholics wish each other at every Mass, I was not at peace. I viewed porn on the internet regularly, I wasn't the husband or brother or son I should have been, I was too focused on work and financial investments. I could go on, but I won't bore you. Even though I was making bad choices and was not at peace, I was super-prepared to find peace

> ﯼﯿ
> ## ...there were a small number of things that in getting them right, completely changed my life...just 5 things.
> ﯼﯿ

as someone who grew up in the Catholic Church. As a Cradle Catholic, you too have been prepared to find a deep sense of peace as indicated by the worksheet on the previous page, even if you don't feel especially prepared.

It turns out that with my Cradle Catholic preparation, there were a small number of things that in getting them right, completely changed my life. I believe that it was just five things. Not a lot of things to get right, just five.

These five things, what I call the "5 BIG IDEAS for Cradle Catholics", were learned in some cases over the course of a few years, in other cases in a few short months or even in just one week. The BIG IDEAS all came together to transform me.

I believe the 5 BIG IDEAS can be the basis for transforming the life of anyone who grew up Catholic, any Cradle Catholic. This could be you or someone you know. It doesn't matter whether you're still in the Catholic Church, whether you've migrated to another faith community, or you're not affiliated with any faith organization. The 5 BIG IDEAS are universal, and apply to all Catholics and

> ﯼﯿ
> ## ...the 5 BIG IDEAS can be the basis for transforming the life of anyone who grew up Catholic, any Cradle Catholic.
> ﯼﯿ

anyone really. While the underlying messages apply to anyone, this book focuses on helping Cradle Catholics in their transformation to find a deep sense of peace, and is written especially for Cradle Catholics.

* * *

Disclaimer: What this Book is Not...and What it Is

This book is not intended to convince anyone to leave the Catholic Church. On the other hand, it's not intended to convince anyone to return to the Catholic Church who has left. I believe that you can find a deep sense of peace and remain in the Catholic Church. I also believe that you can find a deep sense of peace outside the Catholic Church.

> ℅℃℞
>
> **This book is not intended to convince anyone to leave the Catholic Church...it is not intended to convince anyone to return to the Catholic Church who has left either.**
>
> ℅℃℞

As your understanding of the 5 BIG IDEAS increases, you may find some things done in your Catholic church a distraction, irrelevant, or not in keeping with the teachings of Jesus, but you probably won't find anything so distracting or irrelevant to justify moving to another faith community outside the Catholic Church. If you do, then move.

You can find the same distractions, irrelevance, and stuff not in keeping with the teachings of Jesus at Mainline Protestant churches, Evangelical churches, and at your local Starbucks, but that doesn't necessarily mean you should stop going to any of those either if you do go to them.

You may be sickened or personally affected by the priest abuse scandal but that too is not necessarily a reason to leave the church. Whether you choose to stay or leave, that choice is up to you. God's Grace knows no limits, so be careful not to limit the Grace of God. While it may be difficult to imagine God's Grace reaching someone with a millstone hung around their neck as they are thrown into the sea[11], with God, all things are possible[12]. Don't put artificial limits on what God can do.

> ℅℃℞
>
> **You can be a follower of Jesus in or out of the Catholic Church, that is your decision to make.**
>
> ℅℃℞

There's a silver lining to that very dark cloud. Think of how many people have been freed up by the scandal to question the church, to question their own beliefs, to write books such as this. There was a time when many people thought priests, bishops and the Pope don't sin. Of course they're human and do[13]. Everyone in the Catholic Church now knows that. The priest abuse scandal is an example of how God can even turn human

---

11 Gospel of Matthew, Chapter 18, verse 6, Jesus says: "Whoever causes one of these little ones who believe in me to sin, it would be better for him to have a great millstone hung around his neck and to be drowned in the depths of the sea." A similar verse can be found in the Gospels of Mark and Luke (Mark 9:42 and Luke 17:2, NAB-RE)

12 Jesus said that "with God all things are possible" as retold in the Gospel of Matthew 19:26.

13 Pope Francis said as much: "we are all weak and we are all sinners" (General Audience, November 13, 2013, St. Peter's Sq.)

brokenness and mistakes to His purpose for good. My own mistakes and brokenness are another example. God can turn your brokenness and your mistakes to His purpose also.

You can find a deep sense of peace in or out of the Catholic Church, that's your decision to make. While our family is actively involved in a non-denominational Christian church in Colorado, and we readily admit that the members of that church were the hands and feet of Jesus in our transformation, I still periodically attend Mass at a local Catholic parish, and other Catholic parishes. After reading and putting into practice the 5 BIG IDEAS, you should be open to participating in any Christian congregation's worship service, Catholic, Lutheran, Methodist, Evangelical, Quaker, Mennonite, Amish, etc. If you take on the 5 BIG IDEAS, you'll be uniquely qualified to help other Cradle Catholics also find a path to a deep sense of peace, and should be open to opportunities to do that as they arise.

This book is not a book written by a priest, or by a Bishop, or by a righteous Catholic trying to win you over to becoming a fervent Catholic, to becoming "more Catholic." I've read some of those books and the key message is typically something like: "you would be better off if you went to confession regularly", "come back to the Eucharist (Communion), it's what you're longing for" or some other similar encouragement. That may or may not be the case, but that is not what this guide is about, and those

> ೫೦೧೪
>
> **This book *is* a guide written by a sinner who found a path back to God, and as a result found a deep sense of peace and a joy for life he has never before known.**
>
> ೫೦೧೪

encouragements to be more Catholic definitely won't help you until you've taken on the 5 BIG IDEAS.

This book is not written by a gifted writer who will delight you and entertain you. While the author and the collaborators have labored to make this book clear and engaging, look past the flaws in writing and presentation to see and understand the guidance and insights that can dramatically change your life.

This book *is* a guide written by a sinner who, with the help of others, found a path back to God, and as a result stumbled upon a deep sense of peace and a joy for life. The sinner would like to show you that path so that you can find that same deep sense of peace and joy for life.

* * *

How to Read and Make Use of the Plans in this Book

There's no one right way to read this book, but it generally flows in a way that's intended to be most helpful to you. The order of the 5 BIG IDEAS is intentional.

You can work through the book on your own or in a group. If you work in a group you can take turns leading or make use of a facilitator.

Focus on understanding the first three BIG IDEAS first, tailoring a simple plan for each based on your circumstances, and implementing each plan. As you focus on the first three BIG IDEAS, you can work on more than one at the same time or focus on one at a time, whatever works best for you. It doesn't make much sense to invest time in the fourth or the fifth BIG IDEA until you've made significant progress in the first three.

Activities and a simple plan are provided for each BIG IDEA based on my own experience and my experience working with a few others to help them in their faith journey. I didn't have "activities" to work through. Everyone has a different amount of structure they are comfortable with, so use them as is or just see through to the purpose of the activity and do what you need to do to accomplish the same goal. Resources that I would consider highly effective are listed and I would strongly encourage you to make use of them. You may not find them as effective for you as they were for me, but you won't know that until you've used them. A few resources that may or may not be helpful to you, resources that I wouldn't consider essential for *everyone*, are listed as "optional" or are mentioned in a chapter. Some of these optional resources may be very helpful to you personally, so consider them as you tailor and put into motion a plan that is best for you. Each simple plan has blank rows to enable you to make use of other resources that present themselves to you.

Some of the resources may be available at your local library, so check there first. If the resource is something you'd like to have in your personal library, you can purchase it after checking out a copy from the library. All of the resources are available from Amazon.com and other retailers. Some are available "used" on Amazon and can be purchased for much less used than new. I've purchased hundreds of used books from Amazon in the past five years and have never been disappointed with a book listed in "good", "very good", or "like new" condition. If you buy books used on Amazon, be careful with books listed in "acceptable" condition. Typically I've been disappointed with "acceptable" books unless the book was the only available copy.

Like anything in life, the most important step and the most difficult step to take is the first one. The others are easy and will just flow. So just get started.

BIG IDEA #1:
Understand and Accept Grace

Traditional Catholic Prayer Before Meals:

Bless us, O Lord

and these Thy gifts,

which we are about to receive,

from Thy bounty,

through Christ our Lord,

Amen.

BIG IDEA #1: Understand and Accept Grace

As a family, we prayed the prayer on the previous page before *every* dinner. We called it "Grace", as in "let's say Grace before we eat".

We still recite this prayer before meals. Sometimes I'm the only person at the table who has any significant link to the Catholic Church. I wonder what the non-Cradle Catholics must think. We recently went to dinner with Ken, the Pastor of our church, and Melissa, one of our boys and I led with this prayer before we ate. While Ken is someone who prays often, that may have been the first time Ken recited that particular prayer. Melissa and our boys have recited it hundreds of times over the last five or six years. I've recited it more than ten thousand times.

It's a beautiful prayer, and it conveys a lot in a few words. As a familiar prayer that is recited repetitively, we need to be careful not to rush through it, we need to be careful that the younger people with us are reciting the right words over time. We need to care enough to take the time with the younger ones over a longer period to see that they understand the meaning of the words, and the meaning *behind and around* the words.

When we visit family in the summer in New Jersey we recite the exact same prayer (except my brother Mike, if he is present, sometimes adds at the end, "and please bless [insert name of young child at table], he's doing the best that he can". It's sure to get a few laughs from those at table, and a puzzled look, but sense of importance, from the child who is receiving this special blessing from Daddy or Uncle Mike, depending.

> ℘CՅ
> **This simple prayer before meals was my understanding of the meaning of Grace for most of my life. A prayer said by all before meals. I was wrong.**
> ℘CՅ

This simple prayer before meals was my understanding of the meaning of Grace for most of my life. A prayer said by all before meals. I was wrong.

I also understood Grace to be a person's name. I've known a few people named Grace, but I didn't understand the meaning and importance of their name.

I have come to understand that Grace, God's forgiveness of us, is one of the core pillars of Christianity, but that understanding has come to me only relatively recently in life. Everything in this guidebook flows from Grace, so it only makes sense to start there. If you don't really understand Grace, nothing else matters. You need to stop, and develop an understanding of Grace. This chapter and the recommended action plan at the end is designed to help you do just that. Don't settle for a basic or passing understanding of Grace, become an expert, become a connoisseur, dive deep. Grace is the heart, the core of it all: Jesus, the Bible, Christianity, everything hangs off Grace.

But how, as a Catholic, did I not understand the meaning and importance of Grace? Why do many Cradle Catholics not understand the meaning and importance of Grace?

I'm not sure, but here's what I think is the reason many Cradle Catholics don't have a fine appreciation for God's Grace, why I didn't have a fine appreciation for God's Grace. It's not that it's not there. It is. It's all around, but Grace is surrounded by so much noise and distraction that it's missed. Also, I don't think it's taught. I can't recall in all of the Catholic school religious instruction that I've had in grade school and high school (and the CCD classes I had in grade school and high school) that God's Grace was ever specifically taught. If it was, I missed it. I missed it and you probably missed it too.

Understanding and accepting God's Grace is the first of the 5 BIG IDEAS. I'll share with you my journey to come to understand Grace, and then accept it. You can use the same approach to come to understand Grace yourself and accept the gift. Then you'll be ready to take on BIG IDEA #2: Forgive Others – *No Exceptions*, simply passing on what God has given you on to others.

* * *

How I Came to Understand Grace

ℰꙅℭꙅ

I never heard anyone describe Grace as something that was a gift. To me.

ℰꙅℭꙅ

The way I came to understand Grace is so unlikely, that there's no other reasonable explanation except that God had a hand in it. A few years ago within the space of a few days, the topic of Grace came up in a variety of places all at once. It was the subject of a radio discussion. Someone mentioned it in passing. It showed up in an article I read. In four or five places the topic of Grace arose. The coincidences of Grace coming up in that many places in so short a time made me suspicious and even laugh. Ok, God, I can take a hint, what exactly is Grace? I did a little digging. I googled "Grace" and of course the wikipedia entry was one of the first to pop up, so I read the entry describing "Christian Grace"...

from wikipedia.org:[14]

> In Western Christian theology, **grace** has been defined, not as a created substance of any kind, but as "the love and mercy given to us by God because God desires us to have it, not because of anything we have done to earn it", "the condescension or benevolence shown by God toward the human race". It is understood by Christians to be a spontaneous gift from God to man - "generous, free and totally unexpected and undeserved" - that takes the form of divine favor, love, clemency, and a share in the divine life of God.

The wikipedia entry continued, describing the differences in beliefs between Catholics and Protestants.

Some people, especially academics, look down their nose at wikipedia as it is, they believe, not as rigorous as an edited encyclopedia. Many of the high school students I work with have been taught not to trust the information found in wikipedia. That teaching doesn't help them. I find wikipedia helpful: it's quick to access, I find it highly accurate, and it's easily accessible[15]. That wikipedia entry opened my eyes. The concept of Grace was simple – I could understand it right away, but it was new to me. Of course I knew the story of Jesus, the son of God, coming to earth, teaching and ministering, suffering and dying on the cross, rising to life. But I had never heard anyone describe Grace as something that was a gift. To me (and to you). It was something I could not – and did not have to – earn. It was simply a gift to accept, from a God who loves me.

This description of Grace was a big deal, a very big deal. It is the biggest of BIG IDEAS of any kind. I spent most of my life thinking (incorrectly) that I was not a sinner. Later I came to realize, accept, and

---

14 Retrieved from http://en.wikipedia.org/wiki/Grace_(Christianity) on August 4, 2014.

15 I've spent more time in the business world than the academic world, so I lean more toward results over neatness and order.

confront the sins of my past and the sins of the present. Once I honestly confronted my sins, I felt that I had sinned so badly and made such a muck of my life and the life of others that I could never get "clean", never overcome the sins of the past. I felt like I had dug myself into a hole so deep that I could never possibly work myself out of it. This description of Grace was warm and welcoming. All is not lost. I wanted to learn more.

I went to Amazon and looked for books that described Grace. I ordered a few books that focused on Grace. When they came, I mined them for a better understanding of Grace. I didn't find anything that was much help. One book that was mildly helpful was a book that reprinted Charles Spurgeon's sermons, *Grace, God's Unmerited Favor*. Spurgeon was a preacher from the 1800s[16].

I was intrigued by the song *Amazing Grace*. Someone had put to words a description of the incredible gift of Grace. I listened to the song performed by a variety of artists. LeAnn Rimes' a capella version is my favorite, and I meditated on the concept of Grace over the course of a few months, listening to the song over and over. I still listen to LeAnn's recording.

The song interested me so I did a little research and came to know the background story of its writing. *Amazing Grace* was written by a former Captain of a Slave Ship who came to terms with the evil he perpetuated, and wrote the song based on his own experience. I watched the 2007 DVD, *Amazing Grace*, directed by Michael Apted. The movie focuses on the work of William Wilberforce, played by Welsh actor Ioan Guffeld, to abolish England's involvement in the slave trade. Albert Finney brings John Newton to life as Wilberforce's Pastor, the author of the lyrics to *Amazing Grace*.

* * *

---

16 The Spurgeon book was somewhat helpful, but as a preacher from the 1800s, the style of writing is a little dense. Check out the book if you're interested, but I don't consider it a critical resource to my understanding and accepting God's Grace. It may be available in your library or you can order it from Amazon or elsewhere for about $8. Also check out www.spurgeon.org, an online archive of the preacher's sermons. It's a little challenging to find what you're looking for on the site, but there's a treasure trove of material that makes poking around worthwhile. Go to www.spurgeon.org/all_of_g.htm

What is Grace?

Over time, I developed a better understanding of Grace, a better appreciation for Grace. Here is my regular person, non-academic understanding of Grace:

We have all sinned, every one of us – me, you, your favorite priest growing up, every Bishop and every Pope. Sin distances us from God. Yet, His love for us remains.

God loves us more than we can comprehend, God also knows of our sin. There are no secrets from God.

God sent his son, Jesus, into the world to suffer and die in payment for our sins – sins of our past, sins of our present, and sins we have yet to commit. This is the ultimate "pay it forward" act (where do you think Oprah got the idea?).

God is the initiator of His Grace. He sent Jesus to suffer and die for our sins two thousand years ago for us right now, and last week, and ten years ago and next week, and ten years from now. The hard part has been done. Our role is to understand Grace and accept Grace as the incredible gift that it is. "Gospel" is Greek for "Good News". Grace, God's forgiveness of my sins and your sins and everyone's sins who understands and accepts Grace is certainly good news.

There's nothing for us to do other than to accept God's forgiveness, as the debt for our sin has already been paid for by Jesus' suffering and death by crucifixion.

We cannot "earn" Grace by doing enough good to outweigh the bad, so get off that treadmill. Grace is a gift to accept just like gifts at birthdays are accepted.

There's no limit to God's Grace, there is nothing you can do that would be outside the bounds of what God can handle.

While we cannot earn Grace, and it is a gift from God freely given to us, God does expect us to pass Grace along and forgive others who have hurt us, to pass on His Grace that we receive to others. If we don't forgive others, God doesn't forgive us. This is the "fine print" to this incredible gift. I call it the "forgiveness clause" (more on this in BIG IDEA #2). This requirement embodies deep wisdom, it's not to punish us in some way. Being in a state of unforgiveness imprisons us.

The gift of Grace allows us to move forward in our life, freeing us up for undergoing a transformation or rebirth that God wants for each of us sinners, and enables us then to become followers and then disciples of Jesus, who has identified very specific instructions for how we should live (BIG IDEA #3).

Rather than being stuck in the past, we are called to live fully, to live abundantly, to have a joy for life, and to be in a state of peace in the present (BIG IDEA #4).

God does expect us to "repent" or "turn away from" our past sins, and over time He helps us do that, what some call "sanctification". It's a process, not an event. It takes time. He only asks us to turn away. For sins that are deeply rooted in habit and in which we might still cling to, we need to have the humility to ask God for help.

* * *

That's it. It's not complicated, but you must understand what Grace is before you can accept it. God's Grace is actually simple to understand, but powerful. This summary is an imperfect start at helping you understand God's Grace, but it gives you a jump on developing your own understanding.

How I Missed BIG IDEA #1 as a Cradle Catholic

(and how you may have missed it too)

How is it possible that I missed understanding and accepting Grace? Here's how:

Reason #1: "Grace" is used to mean a few different things in the Catholic Church, not just God's forgiveness of us, through Jesus' sacrificial suffering and death.

For me, there was a lot of "noise and confusion" surrounding God's Grace in the Catholic Church. The Catholic Church in its use of the word Grace extends the concepts of Grace beyond this initial gift. It's not wrong, but it did cause me to miss BIG IDEA #1, and I think it may cause many others to miss it too. The Catholic Church's broader definition of Grace extends beyond God's forgiveness of our sins and Jesus' sacrifice for us. Grace as a concept in the Catholic Church also includes the assistance God gives us to grow in our faith after we have accepted the gift of forgiveness. Another source of confusion related to the word "Grace" for me and probably for other Cradle Catholics, is using "Grace" as the name of a prayer of thanksgiving and blessing before meals (see the prayer at the start of this chapter), as in "let's say Grace".

Reason #2: The Updated Catechism of the Catholic Church came out only recently, and is probably not widely understood by those within the Catholic Church

I doubt Christians of any type would take issue with the definition of Grace in the recently updated version of the Catholic Catechism (CCC 1996 through 1999) that came out in the 1990s. I doubt Martin Luther himself, or John Wesley, or John Calvin would take issue with the definition of Grace in the updated Catechism. For anyone who's sinned, Grace is huge, it's an incredible, welcome gift. For anyone who has sinned deeply it's astounding. It really is a BIG IDEA, and the biggest idea of the 5 BIG IDEAS, the "gateway" BIG IDEA. The description of God's Grace in the new version of the Catechism I understand and is a big idea. I'm not sure I understand God's Grace based on the definition in the Baltimore Catechism. If everyone in the Catholic Church's understanding of Grace was based on the definition of Grace in the Baltimore Catechism, that would be one of the reasons I missed BIG IDEA #1. If I don't understand it by reading the document I probably won't understand someone explaining the document to me.

* * *

Reason #3: My own flawed perception of the sacrament of Reconciliation

The Sacrament of Reconciliation[17], or "going to Confession" as many Catholics refer to the sacrament, was a source of confusion for me about the meaning of Grace. After confessing my sins to the Priest in attendance, I was always given an assignment, typically of praying a certain number of prayers. While the intent was pure, the impression this left on me, subconsciously as I never stopped to think about it, was that I had to do some work – usually prayer – in order to get back in good standing with God. I perceived, incorrectly, that I was earning my way to forgiveness. To the extent that the same impression is left with millions or billions of other Catholics who participate in the sacrament of Reconciliation, the sacrament, as it is currently designed and practiced, could be refined (assuming it hasn't been already). My experience of the sacrament was too "transactional". What's missing from the sacrament is the *explicit* recognition by everyone involved that salvation is impossible on our own, but with God it's possible. The sacrament was also flawed, in my experience[18], in that there was no focus on the requirement to forgive others[19], but that's discussed in the next chapter.

Reason #4: The Lamb of God, recited at every Mass, is a mashup of two very different things (forgiveness of sins and healing), and gave me the wrong impression of God's Grace

Every time you went to Mass, before Communion, you and the entire Church recited or sang the *Agnus Dei* or *Lamb of God*. Here are the words in English:

> Lamb of God
> *Lamb of God, you take away the sins of the world, have mercy on us,*
> *Lamb of God you take away the sins of the world, have mercy on us,*
> *Lamb of God, you take away the sins of the world, grant us peace.*

I've recited these words more than a thousand times, but the words gave me the wrong impression of God's Grace.

Jews sacrificed animals, lambs included, to God as a form of honor to God. Animal sacrifice goes all the

---

17 This sacrament was called "Penance" when I was a young student in Catholic elementary school in the 1970s. The sacrament has been revised over the course of my childhood. Many Catholic writers encourage readers to go to Confession regularly to deepen their relationship with God. I think they are on the right track, but based on personal experience would humbly recommend people work to understand the meaning of Grace and accept it. They can do that with a priest or pastor who will be sure to guide them.

18 The sacrament of reconciliation may have been revised since I last participated in it, so make your own assessment of how your experience with the sacrament is aligned with the clear teachings of grace, God's forgiveness of us, as described by Jesus, Paul, and others in the New Testament.

19 When I first learned of the *requirement* to forgive I was shocked. In all my years in the Catholic Church, I had never heard anyone describe forgiveness as a requirement, but it is clearly there in Matthew 6:14-15. I was in a meeting of men at a Catholic Church in Denver earlier this week and one of the participants spoke of studying the requirement to forgive, so Jesus' teaching is getting out there.

way back to Cain and Abel, the sons of Adam and Eve in the Book of Genesis in the Bible. Jesus, was the Lamb of God, meaning he was God's sacrifice. He was sacrificed for our sins, like animals were sacrificed by Jews to "atone" or make up for their sins. That is the meaning of "Lamb of God". God sacrificed Jesus for our sins.

Think about the link between Jesus, God's sacrifice, and our sins. The result is God's Grace, or "Mercy", on us. You and me. That's a BIG IDEA. God's Grace and it was right there every week at mass. You and I recited the words without really understanding them, or if we did understand, we didn't stop to appreciate them.

The basis for the Lamb of God is John the Baptist's description of Jesus to those around him as Jesus came towards John:

> *The next day John saw Jesus coming toward him and said,*
> *"Look, the Lamb of God, who takes away the sins of the world!"*
> *Gospel of John 1:29 (NIV)*

Unfortunately, "have mercy on us" is tacked on to the end of two of the lines, a mash-up of two completely different things in the Gospels: forgiveness of sins and healings. "Have mercy on us" is an allusion to Jesus' healing of the blind (one blind person in Luke 18:37-43 and two blind people in Matthew 9:27-29). Jesus clearly stated in the Gospels that his physical healings were different than forgiving sins.[20] The mashup has the effect of making it seem that God's gift of Grace is something we have to beg for, we must ask God. Does it seem right to ask for gifts we've already received? I don't think it does. We just receive a gift and are thankful for what we receive as gifts.

The Lamb of God was one reason I didn't understand God's Grace, it gave me the wrong impression of God's Grace. The Lamb of God was introduced by Pope Sergius I in about the year 700 A.D, so while it has been a part of the Mass for a long time – 1,300 years – it doesn't trace its roots back to the *early* Church. Sergius I was Syrian and the Agnus Dei was a chant that the Syrian Church used. Over the centuries, many composers set the Lamb of God words to music, and many compositions are beautiful and moving. Enjoy them but just keep in mind that God's forgiveness of sins through Jesus and Jesus' healings are different things, and that God has *already* had mercy on you in the suffering and death of Jesus. While both forgiveness and healings are impressive, God's forgiveness of our sins through Jesus' suffering and death is infinitely more impressive than physical healings, and God's forgiveness has an eternal impact, while physical healings have an impact in time that is rounding error in comparison to eternity.

* * *

---

20 If you read the Gospel of Mark or watch the Max McLean DVD of Mark you will develop an understanding of how Jesus saw healings and forgiveness of sins. Jesus believed forgiveness of sins was much more important than healing physical ailments, and much more impressive. He also taught that they are not related: you are not blind because you or one of your parents sinned, as some at the time believed.

Taking on BIG IDEA #1: Understand and Accept Grace
A Simple Plan that Works

The plan below is designed to help you take on BIG IDEA #1. It's based on my personal experience of what works. Check off tasks as you complete them using the column at the right. The tasks are in an order that seems to make sense, but do them in any order that works for you. The rows at the end are for additions to the plan that you may have, if any. The pages that follow the plan include information and activities mentioned in the plan that will help you complete it.

Task	Description	Investment	Complete?
Read	**Read the "Grace (Christian)" wikipedia.org entry** This is a great first step to developing an understanding of Grace. Many academics look down upon wikipedia as a source of information that, they believe, is not to be relied upon. I believe wikipedia is a great source of information, and I recommend you make use of it to develop an understanding of Grace.	10-20 minutes	☐
Read	**Read the Bible Passages that describe God's Grace** [see Biblical passages later in this chapter]	1 hour	☐
Activity	**Complete Activity 1.1: God's Grace in My Own Words**	10-20 minutes	☐
Activity	**Complete Activity 1.2: *Amazing Grace* Musical Study**	varies	☐
Activity	**Complete Activity 1.3: Paul & Peter's Use of the Word "Grace" Study**	30 minutes	☐
Read	**Read *The Jesuit Guide to (Almost) Everything: A Spirituality for Real Life* by James Martin, S.J. (book)** [see description later in this chapter]	3 – 6+ hours $11 (paperback) $20 (hardcover) check your library	☐
Find	**A Handful of Christians Who Will Help You Grow** (likely in another parish or congregation) [see description later in this chapter]	A few weeks or months	☐
Activity	**Complete Activity 1.4: Accepting God's Gift of Grace**	a moment	☐

Task	Description	Investment	Complete?
▶ **DVD** ▶ **Watch** (optional)	***Amazing Grace* (DVD)** The movie "Amazing Grace" (DVD) describes the work of William Wilberforce in liberating Great Britain from the slave trade. The best part of the movie is the cameo appearance of the actor Albert Finney in the role of John Newton, the author of the lyrics to the hymn *Amazing Grace*. Understanding the circumstances of Newton's life is helpful in understanding God's Grace. While watching the movie is not critical to understanding God's Grace, it was helpful to me.	3 hours $4 (new) check your library	☐
			☐
			☐
			☐
PLAN TOTAL		6- 12 hours $0.00 – 33.00	☐

RESOURCE: The Bible (key passages describing God's Grace)

The best way to develop your understanding of Grace is to read and study the Gospels and Paul's Letters that describe Grace. The passages below are what I believe to be the best Biblical passages that can help you understand Grace. Use this page and the check boxes below to track your progress in reading and studying these key passages describing God's Grace, each of which you can read on the following pages:

☐   **God's Grace as described by Jesus in His "Parable of the Prodigal Son"** (Luke 15: 11-32)

☐   **God's Grace as described by Paul in Ephesians** (Ephesians 2:4-10)

☐   **God's Grace as described by Paul in Romans** (Romans 3:21-25)

☐   **God's Grace and the Rich Young Man** (Matthew 19: 23-26)

☐   **God's Grace at the Last Supper** (Matthew 26: 27-28)

☐   **God's Grace after the Resurrection** (Luke 24:45-48)

☐   **God's Grace described by John the Baptist** (John 1: 29-31)

☐   **God's Grace described by Jesus, freeing people from the slavery of sin** (John 8:34-36)

☐   **God's Grace as described by Paul in Titus** (Titus 3:3-7)

Note: Most of the passages below are included within the Catholic Lectionary[21] for Sundays and Major Feasts and you have probably heard them read at Mass. Two of the Gospel passages and one verse from the Titus passage are not in the Sunday and Major Feast Lectionary. So, if you've never read and studied the Bible outside the Mass they will be new to you. Each passage that is excluded from the Sunday and Major Feast Lectionary and which you may not have ever heard is labeled:

"* NOT READ AT SUNDAY MASS ***".**

* * *

---

21   The Lectionary is the predefined list of Bible readings that are read at Mass and are on a three year cycle. The Lectionary is described in more detail in BIG IDEA #3.

God's Grace as described by Jesus in His "Parable of the Prodigal Son"
(Luke 15: 11-32, NIV, emphasis added)
Jesus' parable describes the depth of God's forgiveness of us. You can see where some of the lyrics from the song *Amazing Grace* came from (bold typeface below).:

Jesus continued: "There was a man who had two sons. The younger one said to his father, 'Father, give me my share of the estate.' So he divided his property between them.

"Not long after that, the younger son got together all he had, set off for a distant country and then squandered his wealth in wild living. After he had spent everything, there was a severe famine in that whole country, and he began to be in need. So he went and hired himself out to a citizen of that country, who sent him to his fields to feed pigs. He longed to fill his stomach with the pods that the pigs were eating, but no one gave him anything.

"When he came to his senses, he said, 'How many of my father's hired men have food to spare, and here I am starving to death! I will set out and go back to my father and say to him: Father I have sinned against heaven and against you. I am no longer worthy to be called your son; make me like one of your hired men.' So he got up and went to his father.

"But while he was still a long way off, his father saw him and was filled with compassion for him; he ran to his son threw his arms around him and kissed him.

ജ︎ര︎

"...Let's have a feast and celebrate.

For this son of mine was dead and is alive again;

he was lost and is found."

ജ︎ര︎

"The son said to him, 'Father, I have sinned against heaven and against you. I am no longer worthy to be called your son.'

"But the father said to his servants, 'Quick! Bring the best robe and put it on him. Put a ring on his finger and sandals on his feet. Bring the fattened calf and kill it. Let's have a feast and celebrate. For this son of mine was dead and is alive again; he was lost and is found.' So they began to celebrate.

"Meanwhile the older son was in the field. When he came near the house, he heard music and dancing. So he called one of the servants and asked him what was going on. 'Your brother has come,' he replied, 'and your father has killed the fattened calf because he has him back safe and sound.'

"The older brother became angry and refused to go in. So his father went out and pleaded with him. But he answered his father, 'Look! All these years I've been slaving for you and never disobeyed your orders. Yet you never gave me even a young goat so I could celebrate with my friends. But when this son of yours who has squandered your property with prostitutes comes home, you kill the fattened calf for him!'

"'My son,' said the father, 'you are always with me, and everything I have is yours. But we had to celebrate and be glad, because this brother of yours was dead and is alive again; **he was lost and is found.**'

My Experience: In turning away from the life I had lived, just in the turning, God came to me. I just turned in His direction and he provided me with incredible people and resources to help me grow. Implied in this parable is God's promise to come running to us if we just resolve to go back to Him. He comes running to us before we even get to him. That is exactly what God did for me. You just need to make the turn.

God's Grace as described by Paul in Ephesians (Ephesians 2:4-10, NAB-RE, emphasis added)
Paul describes Grace, God's forgiveness of our sins, as a gift. It is not something we can earn by doing good deeds:

ℰ෬

**For by grace you have been saved through faith,
and this is not from you; it is a gift of God;
it is not from works, so no one may boast.**

ℰ෬

But God, who is rich in mercy, because of the great love he had for us, even when we were dead in our transgressions, brought us to life with Christ (by grace you have been saved), raised us up with him, and seated us with him in the heavens in Christ Jesus, that in the ages to come he might show the immeasurable riches of his grace in his kindness to us in Christ Jesus.

For by grace you have been saved through faith, and this is not from you; it is the gift of God; it is not from works, so no one may boast.

<u>My Experience</u>: When I first came to understand Grace, this was the only Biblical passage I was aware of describing Grace. For a Cradle Catholic, if you are going to have just one passage from the Bible to understand Grace, this passage would be it.

* * *

God's Grace as described by Paul in Romans (Romans 3:21-25, NAB-RE, emphasis added)
Paul describes the fact that all are broken and have sinned. Jesus paid restitution (atonement) for our sins:

But now a righteousness from God, apart from the law, has been made known, to which the Law and the Prophets testify. This righteousness from God comes through faith in Jesus Christ to all who believe.

> ෴
>
> **...for all have sinned and fall short of the glory of God, and are justified freely by his grace through the redemption that came by Christ Jesus. God presented him as a sacrifice of atonement.**
>
> ෴

There is no difference, for all have sinned and fall short of the glory of God, and are justified freely by his grace through the redemption that came by Christ Jesus. God presented him as a sacrifice of atonement.

* * *

God's Grace and the Rich Young Man (Matthew 19: 23-26, emphasis added)
Jesus describes the fact that none of us can be saved except through God's forgiveness, His Grace. Even rich people, who the disciples thought could do anything they wanted, couldn't be saved on their own:

*** NOT READ AT SUNDAY MASS ***
Then Jesus said to his disciples, "I tell you the truth, it is hard for a rich man to enter the kingdom of heaven. Again I tell you, it is easier for a camel to go through the eye of a needle than for a rich man to enter the kingdom of God."

> **"Who then can be saved?"**
> **"With man this is impossible, but with God all things are possible."**

When the disciples heard this, they were greatly astonished and asked, "Who then can be saved?"

Jesus looked at them and said, "With man this is impossible, but with God all things are possible."

God's Grace at the Last Supper (Matthew 26: 27-28, emphasis added)
Jesus linked His death to the forgiveness of our sins, a new agreement between God and people:

> **"This is my blood of the covenant, which is poured out for many for the forgiveness of sins."**

Then he took the cup, gave thanks and offered it to them, saying, "Drink from it, all of you. This is my blood of the covenant, which is poured out for many for the forgiveness of sins."

Cradle Catholics will recognize that this passage is part of what the priest says at Mass before Communion. Consider how these words apply to you personally.

God's Grace after the Resurrection (Luke 24:45-48, emphasis added)
After Jesus rose from the dead, he appeared to two of the disciples on the road to Emmaus. He ate dinner with them and explained what had happened:

> ঙ৩৵
> **"This is what is written: the Christ will suffer and rise from the dead on the third day, and repentance and forgiveness of sins will be preached in his name..."**
> ঙ৩৵

Then he opened their minds so they could understand the Scriptures. He told them,

"This is what is written: the Christ will suffer and rise from the dead on the third day, and repentance and forgiveness of sins will be preached in his name to all nations, beginning at Jerusalem. You are witnesses of these things."

God's Grace described by John the Baptist (John 1: 29-31, emphasis added)
During Jesus' time on Earth, animals, including lambs, were slaughtered as sacrifices to God, sometimes as atonement for the sin of the person offering the animal as sacrifice:

The next day John saw Jesus coming toward him and said,

"Look, the Lamb of God, who **takes away the sin of the world**!. This is the one I meant when I said, 'A man who comes after me has surpassed me because he was before me.' I myself did not know him, but the reason I came baptizing with water was that he might be revealed to Israel."

Cradle Catholics will recognize the first verse, "Lamb of God, who takes away the sins of the world," as one that is recited at every Mass.

God's Grace described by Jesus, the bread of life (John 6:47-51)
Jesus described himself as the bread of life. He gave up his body so we might have everlasting life:

> "I tell you the truth, he who believes has everlasting life. I am the bread of life. Your forefathers ate the manna in the desert, yet they died. But here is the bread that comes down from heaven, which a man may eat and not die. I am the the living bread that came down from heaven. If anyone eats of this bread, he will live forever. This bread is my flesh, which I will give for the life of the world."

God's Grace described by Jesus, freeing people from the slavery of sin (John 8:34-36)

> ***** NOT READ AT SUNDAY MASS *****
> Jesus replied, "I tell you the truth, everyone who sins is a slave to sin. Now a slave has no permanent place in the family, but a son belongs to it forever. So if the Son sets you free, you will be free indeed."

* * *

God's Grace as described by Paul in Titus (Titus 3:3-7, NAB-RE, emphasis added)

> ***** NOT READ AT SUNDAY MASS *** (verse 3, verses 4-7 are read)**

> "For we ourselves were once foolish, disobedient, deluded,
> slaves to various desires and pleasures, living in malice and envy,
> hateful of ourselves and hating one another.

> "But when the kindness and generous love of God our savior appeared,
> **not because of any righteous deeds we had done but because of his mercy,**
> he saved us through the bath of rebirth and renewal by the holy Spirit,
> whom he richly poured out on us through Jesus Christ our savior,
> **so that we might be justified by his grace**
> **and become heirs in hope of eternal life."**

* * *

Activity 1.1: God's Grace in My Own Words

How to Complete this Activity: Read the entry for "Grace (Christian)" in wikipedia.org. Read all of the key Bible passages related to God's Grace earlier in this chapter. Read my "non-academic, regular person understanding of Grace" earlier in this chapter. See if you can find additional resources. Record a definition of God's Grace below in your own words. Use additional paper if needed:

A Definition of God's Grace (in my own words)

* * *

Activity 1.2: Amazing Grace Musical Study

How to Complete this Activity:

Step 1: Go to Amazon.com or other music store and preview the various recordings of the song *Amazing Grace* (in the search box type: mp3 Amazing Grace). Pick a recording you like and record the choice below. Purchase the recording.

Amazing Grace Recording
Artist: _____   Album: _____
Song Title: _____

Step 2: Read and study the lyrics to *Amazing Grace* found on the following page. Read about John Newton, the author of the lyrics to *Amazing Grace*. Learn how Newton's life experience caused him to pen the words. Check out the wikipedia entry for John Newton, also check out http://www.anointedlinks.com/amazing_grace.html Make notes below:

John Newton

Steps 3: Listen to your purchased recording of Amazing Grace multiple times. Think about the lyrics as you hear them, reflect on their meaning to John Newton the author and to you. Immerse yourself in the song, listening to it multiple times. Record your listening below if you want, but don't limit yourself. Use the printed lyrics on the next page to read as you listen if that helps you. Check a box each time you listen:

Amazing Grace Listening
☐☐☐☐☐ ☐☐☐☐☐ ☐☐☐☐☐ ☐☐☐☐☐   ☐☐☐☐☐ ☐☐☐☐☐ ☐☐☐☐☐ ☐☐☐☐☐

RESOURCE: *Amazing Grace* (song) by John Newton

Read, study, meditate and listen to performances of *Amazing Grace*, originally titled *Faith's Review and Expectation*.

Amazing Grace[22]

Chorus:	Verses (continued):
Amazing Grace, how sweet the sound, That saved a wretch like me. I once was lost but now am found, Was blind, but now I see. **Verses:** T'was Grace that taught my heart to fear. And Grace, my fears relieved. How precious did that Grace appear The hour I first believed. Through many dangers, toils and snares I have already come; 'Tis Grace that brought me safe thus far and Grace will lead me home. The Lord has promised good to me. His word my hope secures. He will my shield and portion be, As long as life endures.	Yes, when this flesh and heart shall fail, And mortal life shall cease, I shall possess within the veil, A life of joy and peace. The earth shall soon dissolve like snow, The sun forbear to shine; But God, who called me here below, Will be forever mine. **Later composition, anonymous composer:** When we've been there ten thousand years Bright shining as the sun. We've no less days to sing God's praise Than when we've first begun.

A few things jump out at me when I hear the lyrics to *Amazing Grace*:

- I notice in the chorus the link between my wretchedness, my being "lost", and my being found. I was blind to God's Grace for me, now I better understand Grace and have accepted it.

- I notice what first sounds like a paradox related to fear described in the first verse. How can Grace teach "my heart to fear" while also relieving my fears? This relates to having a fear (or love) of God while being freed from all other fears. What seems like a paradox actually makes sense.

- In the third verse, the words "shield and portion be" means that God will protect us ("shield") and provide for our needs ("portion")

- "A life of joy and peace" in the fourth verse I understand to be the direct outcome of my understanding of God's Grace, and acceptance of His gift.

- The last verse was added later by an unknown composer. I like the concept of eternity described by "ten thousand years" elapsing but no less time to "sing God's praise".

---

22 John Newton (1725-1807) and anonymous downloaded from http://www.constitution.org/col/amazing_grace.htm on September 16, 2014 and also from www.annointedlinks.com/amazing_grace.html on July 22, 2015.

Activity 1.3: Paul & Peter's Use of the Word "Grace" Study

How to Complete this Activity: Take notice of the pattern of the use of the word "Grace" in the Bible by the Apostle Paul and by the Apostle Peter at the beginning of each of their letters. Clearly a pattern and clearly important. Record the typical greeting used by Paul and Peter that includes Grace below:

Chapter/Verse	Chapter / Verse	Chapter / Verse
Romans 1: 7	Philippians 1: 1-2	2 Timothy 1: 1-2
1 Corinthians 1: 2-3	Colossians 1: 1-2	Titus 1: 1
2 Corinthians 1: 1-2	1 Thessalonians 1: 1	Philemon 1: 1-3
Galatians 1: 1-3	2 Thessalonians 1: 1-2	1 Peter 1: 1-2
Ephesians 1: 1-2	1 Timothy 1: 1-2	2 Peter 1: 1-2

Paul's Typical Use of the Word Grace

Peter's Typical Use of the Word Grace

* * *

RESOURCE:
A Jesuit Guide to (Almost) Everything
A Spirituality for Real Life
by James Martin, S. J.

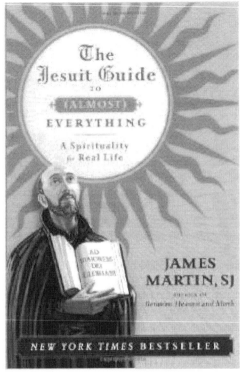

After Melissa and I were told by an organizer of one Catholic parish's Summer Vacation Bible School (VBS) that we couldn't register our young boys for VBS because of our "condition" of both being divorced and remarried, I was livid. I complained to my Mother. She suggested we find "the Jesuits." I didn't know much about the Jesuits, but searched the internet and found there was only one Jesuit parish in all of Colorado. That made the choice easy: we traveled 40 minutes at least once each week to St. Ignatius Loyola parish, East of downtown Denver. The parish welcomed us warmly. Before long, I was helping one of the parishoners in conducting book studies of *A Jesuit Guide to (Almost) Everything* at the church and at a Panera Bread restaurant in downtown Denver.

Book Cover

Right about the time I was learning about God's Grace I was reading this book and leading or helping to lead studies of the book. One very powerful idea in the book is that "God meets you where you are...you do not have to change to engage God...he meets you in whatever circumstances you find yourself when you are ready to engage Him." Once you come to terms with your own sinful nature, the natural assumption is that you somehow need to change before you can accept God's forgiveness. That's not true. Once you understand God's Grace, which has already been paid for by Jesus' suffering and death, you don't need to change in order to accept God's gift. That is a hugely liberating insight that came to me at just the right time.

We're all sinners. Not one of us could change enough to be ready for God's Grace if it were dependent on us. It's not. He comes to us. In addition to that key insight related to God's Grace, the book contains other helpful guidance related to:

- living simply
- praying the Examen, a 500 year-old prayer method of continuous improvement through reflection
- making decisions with God's help (discernment)

I recommend this book to help you understand God's Grace. It's one of a handful of books that I give to others if I think they'll read it, although I have not gifted as many copies of this book as I have *Amish Grace* and *Unconditional* (see next chapter).

* * *

RESOURCE: A Handful of Christians Who Will Help You Grow
(likely in another parish or congregation)

A handful of people worked with Melissa and I to help us grow and as a result transform our lives. John at St. Ignatius Loyola Catholic Church in Denver got us started. Pastor Mark and Miss Carla at Mountainview Christian Church in Highlands Ranch brought us back from the brink of disaster. Paul and Cyndi counseled and coached us.

John is an entrepreneur who got us started on the right path by helping us understand and appreciate some of the deep wisdom of the Jesuits, mainly through James Martin's book described earlier in this chapter. Mark met with me individually or Melissa and I together weekly for a few months. Carla met with Melissa weekly for a few months. When Melissa and I were in crisis, Mark met with us or just with me more than once a week. Paul and Cyndi, as marriage and forgiveness counselors, developed us and helped us break free from the past by showing us how to forgive. When Mark better understood our situation and our challenges, he pulled in Paul and Cyndi who met with us weekly in addition to our meetings with Mark and Carla. Each of these people helped us in our journey. They each invested significant time in my and Melissa's development.

> ୫୦୦ଓ
>
> **...there are many people within the communities of Christians in your area that can dramatically impact your life, for the better. You won't find them any other way than by getting involved in their parish or congregation.**
>
> ୫୦୦ଓ

How did we find each person? Through a community of Christians: a parish or a congregation. One was a member of a Catholic parish, St. Ignatius Loyola. Four were members of a non-denominational Christian church, Mountainview. If you think you don't need to belong to a church, that you don't need "organized religion" you're wrong.

Each of these people we found within a church community. We wouldn't have found any of them if we didn't go to their church.

Lots of detestable things have been done by various religions over the last 2,000 years and the priest abuse scandal is just a recent example. Previous generations witnessed the murder of Muslims and Christians at war with one another (the Crusades), the murder of Amish and Mennonite Christians for choosing to be baptized as adults (the Inquisition), antisemitism, and other acts of violence. As a result, many people avoid organized religion. The fact remains, though, that there are people within the communities of Christians in your area that can dramatically impact your life for the better. You won't find them any other way than by getting involved in their parish or congregation. World-class resources available to you and your family that make use of deep wisdom, helping you solve seemingly unsolvable problems. Problems that can't seem to be solved by buying more stuff or taking drugs or [fill in the blank].

To find each person we had to leave the church of which we were members. We had to take a risk to find each person. We had to be a little uncomfortable for a short while. The jump from the Catholic church that wouldn't register our kids for Vacation Bible School[23] to the Jesuit church wasn't a big jump as we were irritated by our treatment. But there were moments of being uncomfortable, of being uncertain. The payback for taking a little initiative, for taking a little risk was huge as we started to grow in each new church.

The jump from going to the Jesuit Catholic church an hour's drive away to the non-denominational Christian church that we pass by twice a day was a much bigger jump, and more of a challenge, at least for me. It was way outside my comfort zone as a Cradle Catholic, but much easier for Melissa, who wasn't a Cradle Catholic. For me, there was a sense of somehow being disloyal to my family and disloyal to my heritage as a Cradle Catholic:

> **I have deep roots in the Catholic Church and the lines between the Catholic Church and my family are blurred.**

- Growing up, my entire extended family was Catholic: parents, siblings, grandparents, uncles, aunts, and cousins.

- As a young child we would frequently go to Mass with our maternal grandparents at our parish or theirs. Sunday typically meant going to Mass in the morning and having coffee and pastries and sitting around the table afterwards for a few hours. Pretty much every major holiday when we were young – Thanksgiving, Christmas, Easter – was celebrated at my grandparents home after going to Mass. My grandparents didn't have much artwork, but they did have a large reproduction of Salvador Dali's painting *The Last Supper* in the dining room and another large surrealist reproduction of a painting of Jesus over the television where you could see Jesus' heart.

- I was an altar boy. I lit the candles before Mass, rang the bells three times during Mass, wore the black and white cassocks, even held the gold plate with a handle in case any crumbs should fall as people took communion, which was common practice in the 1970s.

- My family made frequent use of Catholic schools. My brother Mike and I went to a Catholic high school in New Jersey: Delbarton. It's run by Benedictine monks that were an offshoot of St. Benedict's Prep in Newark, New Jersey where my Uncle James went to high school. My older brother went to a Catholic high school, Seton Hall Prep, in South Orange, New Jersey. My Dad went to Seton Hall University for college. My sister went to Mount Saint Dominic Academy in West Caldwell, New Jersey. Mom went to Caldwell College on the same campus. Everyone in my family

---

23 As mentioned previously, the Church wouldn't register the boys because Melissa and I are both divorced and remarried.

went to a Catholic high school, college, or both.

- My grandparents would regularly host Sister Rose Vincentia, who we all called "Sister Rose," in their home. Sister Rose was my Mom's grade school principal and grew up in Ireland. While Mom was a star student who I doubt was ever sent to the principal's office for being naughty, her younger brother, Jim, ran away from school one day so she was called into Sister Rose's office to be told what to tell my grandparents about the incident.[24] Later, when my grandfather was diagnosed with a mastoid condition and was hoping to avoid surgery as it could have impacted his ability to work as a truck driver, Jim asked Sister Rose to pray for his dad. She did and my grandfather was cured. That was the start of the relationship that developed between Sister Rose and my grandparents. When Sister Rose moved to live in a nursing home, I drove my grandparents to visit her regularly.

- Mom is active in our home town in New Jersey: St. Catherine of Siena. Mom was on the Parish Council, and is now one of two trustees for that parish, which is like being the legal head of that parish.

The point of all of these anecdotes is to give you a sense of the depth of my roots in the Catholic church. The roots are so deep that the line between the Catholic Church and my family are blurred. Where one ends and the other begins is not clear. Joining a non-Catholic church seemed in a way a betrayal of my family, my heritage, my own experience. But, the one thing that made me go against all of that experience and heritage was the feeling that I was missing something. I wasn't growing and I knew it.

Melissa has brought many blessings into my life, many of which didn't seem like blessings at the particular point in time. Melissa's insistence that we try the non-Catholic churches in our area was one of those blessings. Melissa didn't grow up in any church and after a few years of making the best of trying to understand Jesus, Christianity and the Catholic Church, even trying to make it through RCIA class for converts to Catholicism, Melissa insisted we try some churches that were *not* Catholic (having already tried all of the Catholic churches in the Highlands Ranch area). The church's insistence that Melissa obtain an annulment of her previous marriage before she could be baptized was what put her – and me – over the edge. Can you imagine John the Baptist doing such a thing? Or Phillip[25]? (see BIG IDEA #5 to better understand John and Phillip) Of course not.

> ...I'm deeply grateful (now) for the negative experiences we had with a few churches that led us to try the churches that ended up having a direct hand in our transformation.

---

24 The incident was a minor offense, but it's what connected Sister Rose and my uncle enough to get him to ask her to pray for my grandfather.
25 See Acts of the Apostles 8: 26-39. Phillip baptized the Ethiopian eunuch.

There was great uncertainty in the first few weeks of going to Mountainview, the non-denominational Christian church of which we are now active members. We didn't know what to do in worship. We didn't know anyone at first. There was a lot that was new and there was a lot that was unknown. The bigger jump provided even bigger benefits as the people of that non-denominational Christian church made significant investments of time in our transformation. Looking back, I'm deeply grateful (now) for the negative experiences we had in a few churches that led us to try the churches that ended up having a direct hand in our transformation. I wasn't grateful in the moment. We were angered by the woman who wouldn't register our kids in a Catholic Summer Bible School. We were shocked by the woman in an Evangelical church who said we should leave because our one-year-old was making noise. But in the rearview mirror, these negative experiences really helped us move to where we needed to be to grow. Think about that the next time you are offended by someone in a Christian church of any kind. It might be the not so gentle nudge you need to go somewhere else where you come into contact with the people who will help you grow. It may help you get from where you are to where you need to be.

Within a few weeks of going to Mountainview, Melissa was baptized by immersion, publicly confessing her faith. Not long afterward, our oldest son was baptized. After a period of study of baptism in the Gospels and Acts, I too was baptized even though I was baptized at the tender age of one month in our home church, St. Catherine of Siena (see BIG IDEA #5 Consider Baptism for more detail).

> ℬℭℜ
>
> **...a large number of Cradle Catholics who have stopped going to Mass and stopped being active in a parish feel stuck, as the Catholic Church is all they know.**
>
> ℬℭℜ

I think a large number of Cradle Catholics who have stopped going to Mass and stopped being active in a parish feel stuck, as the Catholic Church is all they know. They too find the lines between their family and the Catholic Church blurred. They feel a sense of disloyalty in trying another Christian congregation outside the Catholic Church. If that sounds like you, realize that there are people out there that are eager to help you grow. Realize that if your Mom or Dad or Grandmother or whoever is the "most Catholic" person in your extended family finds out that you're going to another type of Christian church, they'll probably be thankful that you're going to church, even if it's not a Catholic church.

I don't think it matters what type of congregation you try (non-denominational, Methodist, Lutheran, Baptist, a different Catholic parish, etc.), but I do know that you may need to try a few before you find someone within a particular congregation that is willing to invest time in your development and who has the ability to develop you and help you grow.

If you aren't made to feel welcome, whatever your background, move on, as a group of people who've chosen to follow the teachings of Jesus know that they're called to welcome others. They also know they have a duty to help you develop and grow as a follower of Jesus. They know they're forbidden from judging you, that's God's job.

While everyone's situation is different, here's some advice based on my experience:

- Take responsibility for your growth and development. Be open to help from others, and actively seek out guidance and training from others, but take responsibility for your own development and the growth and development of your family. Work through the BIG IDEAS, make use of

> ℰℛ
> **If you feel you're not growing in your church, find another one...**
> ℰℛ

the recommended resources. Invest in a good study bible. Invest in the recommended books and DVDs described in each BIG IDEA Simple Plan or check them out from the library.

- If you feel you're not growing in your church, find another one. Don't choose a new church based on what is "most similar" to what is familiar. Don't choose a new church based on a denomination being "halfway between" Catholicism and the religion of your spouse. Choose a church based on how you and your family will be supported and developed and given an opportunity to serve others.

- If your Catholic heritage is strong and you struggle with guilt in going to a Protestant or an Evangelical or some other congregation, try all of the Catholic churches within a reasonable commute of where you live. Having tried out or at least visited more than 50 Catholic parishes in at least 10 states and 4 countries over the last few decades, one thing I'm surprised by is the wide diversity across each of the parishes, even within the same geographic area. Each parish has its own strengths and weaknesses. A parish that is a good fit for you may not be a good fit for someone else. Decide for yourself based on your own experience of visiting each parish. While the fundamentals of the Mass are the same across the different parishes, you'll likely find many differences in the ministries offered, many differences in the training provided, and many differences in the opportunities for service to others. Diversity of parishes is a good thing, just as diversity in people is a good thing. Diversity brings strength. Sample them all and pick the best for you and your family. Get involved in more than one parish. Make use of ministries and services and opportunities to serve across multiple parishes.

- As you seek out the parishes in your area, seek out the Deacons in the parish of which there may be one, two or even a few. While the number of priests in the Catholic Church have been in decline in most areas for the past few decades, and as a result some may have responsibilities across multiple parishes, the number of Deacons is growing. A Deacon and his wife may have the time to invest in your growth and development in the same way that Mark and Carla invested in Melissa and my growth and development: one-on-one intense guidance and discipleship for a period of time.

- If you've sampled all of the options for Catholic parishes in your area and you still haven't found one that will grow and support you and your family and will provide you with an opportunity to serve others, look outside the Catholic church to the congregations within a reasonable commute of where you live. Many Cradle Catholics pick a Protestant church that is as similar to what they are accustomed to as possible (Episcopal, etc.) Realize that this works well for some, but for others the same issues they had with the Catholic parishes they will have with churches that are similar. In that case find a congregation that is different: an evangelical church, a non-denominational church, a community church, an Mennonite congregation, a Quaker meeting house, etc. The important thing is to find a group of people in which you and your family can grow and develop and in which you and your family can serve others. Once we decided to look at churches that are not Catholic, we visited two before we found a place we thought we could grow and develop.

- If you find yourself actively involved in a non-Catholic church and are growing, developing and finding opportunities to serve others, if you've worked through the 5 BIG IDEAS and found a deep sense of peace, consider having a secondary relationship with a Catholic parish in your area. As a Cradle Catholic, you have a unique ability to grow and develop others in the Catholic church in a way that others cannot. We have enjoyed the Lenten fish frys at a number of local parishes and have hosted exchange students from Spain through a program run by a local parish. This past weekend, I joined our Spanish exchange student for the Sunday evening Mass at the parish

> ℘ℭ
>
> **I told [the Catholic Priest] that today's Gospel reading was actually funny, and the DVD would help him see the humor...**
>
> ℘ℭ

that sponsors the program. The Gospel reading this past weekend was from Mark. In it, Jesus complains that "Only in his hometown, among his relatives and in his own house is a prophet without honor." Mark continues, "He could not do any miracles there, except lay his hands on a few sick people and heal them" (Mark 6: 1-6). Having watched Max McLean's performance of Mark's Gospel (see BIG IDEA #3 for more detail), I knew that the last line was actually funny, that Jesus could do no miracles there...except heal a few people. I sort of chuckled but looked around and realized that probably not one person in the church understood the humor of Mark's writing. It's easy to miss the humor if you've only read Mark's Gospel, but Max McLean is a gifted and talented professional actor who has studied the Gospel deeply, the humor is clearly there. Once you see the performance you'll say "aah, of course, now I see it".

As our exchange student and I walked back to the car I realized that I had a copy of the Gospel of Mark DVD in the trunk of the car. I grabbed the DVD and approached the priest who was saying goodbye to the parishoners after Mass. I showed him the DVD and asked if he had ever watched it. He hadn't. I told him that it was a word-for-word performance of the entire Gospel of Mark that could be watched in 94 minutes. He was interested. I told him that today's Gospel reading was actually funny, and the DVD would help to see the humor. He accepted the gift of the DVD. Only by going back to a local Catholic Church would that opportunity to help a priest who could in turn help hundreds or thousands of others take place. You have that opportunity as a Cradle Catholic. It doesn't have to be a priest, it could be anyone in the parish.

Realize that even in the time of the Apostle Paul, the early Christian churches of Jerusalem, Ethiopia, Galatia, Ephesus, Rome, and elsewhere were very different and each had different strengths and weaknesses. There was a huge gap between Jewish followers of Jesus and non-Jewish or Gentile followers. The difference between the various congregations of early Christians is bigger than the gap between Catholic parishes, Methodist congregations, and non-denominational Christian congregations. Find the right group of followers of Jesus to help you grow. You'll be richly rewarded for stepping out of your comfort zone of staying where you are, richly rewarded for taking just a little risk, rewarded for being just a little uncomfortable for a short time. If you're not growing and developing and serving, you need to find another home parish or home congregation.

* * *

Activity 1.4: Accepting God's Gift of Grace

How to Complete this Activity: Read the statement below and if you feel that you understand God's Grace and would like to accept His gift of forgiveness, choose to accept the gift. If you would like to memorialize your choice by signing and dating the statement below, do so, although it's not necessary. God will know, whether you memorialize it on a piece of paper or not.

Accepting God's Gift of Grace

Yes, I, _____, choose to accept God's gift of forgiveness for my sins. I realize that Jesus suffered and died by crucifixion in payment for my sins. I understand that the gift cannot be earned, and I gratefully accept the gift.

I understand that God expects me to turn away from my sins (repent), I understand that God expects me to forgive all others who have or will hurt me, and He expects me to take the time to learn Jesus' teachings and put them into practice.

Signed: _____   Date: _____

---

* * *

BIG IDEA #2:
Forgive Others – No Exceptions

For if you forgive others their trespasses,

your heavenly Father will also forgive you;

but if you do not forgive others,

neither will your Father forgive your trespasses.

Gospel of Matthew Chapter 6, verses 14-15

(NRSV-CE, emphasis added)

BIG IDEA #2: Forgive Others – *No Exceptions*

I'm a witness to a miracle. Not the walking on water, creating food, raising someone from the dead type miracle, but a miracle just the same. I've witnessed the miraculous, dramatic change in someone's life who has learned about forgiveness (our requirement to forgive others based on Jesus' teachings) and worked through a process to forgive. The change in their life was dramatic and overnight[26].

> ℘℃ℜ
>
> **Many people, including myself, are surprised to find out that forgiveness isn't just a good idea, it's a *requirement* of all Christians...**
>
> ℘℃ℜ

Many decades of hurt were pent up inside causing them to be a very unhappy person. Unhappy every day. The person was, as I've described it, "walking around angry." That anger would bubble up to rage at times, but typically it was a low level of anger. I had a hunch that the person had a lot of "unforgiveness" in them based on things that they said: "I will never forgive him...", "I will never forgive her...", or based on what they did: recalling how someone has hurt them over and over.

I realized that I needed to learn more about forgiveness and how to actually forgive others, methods of forgiveness. I started with our library and found a handful of books on forgiveness. The more I researched forgiveness the more I realized how important it was.

As a Math and Science tutor, I know that math is not really about fractions or multiplication or long division or what most people think math is about. Math is at its heart the study of patterns, and it's the study and understanding of patterns that makes math so powerful[27]. Understanding patterns can be the difference between one nation succeeding and another failing, understanding patterns can be the difference between one company being profitable and another filing bankruptcy, understanding patterns can be the difference between one person thriving and another person not living up to their potential. I realized that "forgiveness" is a core pattern, if not *the* core pattern of Christianity and the teachings of Jesus[28]. The importance of the pattern of forgiveness cannot be overestimated.

Many people, including myself, are surprised to find out that forgiveness isn't just a good idea, it's a *requirement* of all Christians (Catholics as well as others). No exceptions, regardless of the hurt. If you consider yourself a Jesus follower (which is what every Christian should be) you must follow this command. If someone has hurt you, you have an obligation to forgive them – no exceptions. It matters not what they did, there's no limit to the hurt that must be forgiven.

---

26 Forgiving doesn't mean that the person is cured from anger and done, just that one roadblock in the person's path is removed.

27 I first learned of the importance of finding and making use of patterns by watching the "The Code" and "The Story of Math" DVDs of Professor Marcus du Sautoy, who I believe to be the best math teacher in the world.

28 The other core pattern of Jesus' teachings is "Love." Jesus commands his followers to "Love one another as I have loved you." Love and Forgiveness are the two core patterns of Jesus' teachings.

That doesn't mean that you have to continue being hurt by the person, in fact you should take action to protect yourself. But you're obligated to forgive them, if you yourself are to be forgiven by God.

Forgiving also doesn't mean that you have to keep quiet. If someone is hurting you and you will continue to be in a relationship with them, let them know that what they're doing, or that what they're saying, is hurting you.

Forgiving all others can be a very difficult command of Jesus to follow, especially for anyone who's been deeply hurt. But there's incredible wisdom in the command, wisdom that's not obvious, wisdom that's only apparent after following the command and seeing the results. Consider that this wisdom was given two thousand years ago. This deep wisdom could only come from our designer and creator: God, who knows us intimately.

> ൠ
> **Jesus' requirement
> that we forgive those who have hurt us
> is given in love, not as a punishment...
> unforgiveness in our hearts hurts us...**
> ൠ

Jesus' requirement that we forgive those who've hurt us, everyone who has hurt us without exception, is given in love, not as a punishment. As our designer and creator, Jesus understands that unforgiveness in our hearts hurts us. The evil that was created during the hurt is perpetuated in the unforgiveness. Who's hurt by unforgiveness? Not the person who hurt another, but the person who was hurt. All Christians, all followers of Jesus, should be experts in forgiveness: what it is, what it isn't, how to forgive. The rest of this chapter is designed to get you started on becoming more expert in forgiveness, but continue to develop your understanding over time.

* * *

How I Missed BIG IDEA #2 as a Cradle Catholic
(and you may have too)

How did I miss BIG IDEA #2: Forgive Others – *No Exceptions* as a Cradle Catholic? Here's how:

Reason #1: Matthew 6:14-15 is excluded from the Sunday Gospel readings

Jesus clearly commanded his followers to forgive others, without exception. Jesus is quoted in Matthew 6:14-15 reiterating the requirement to forgive all others, without exception, after describing the requirement in the Our Father, or Lord's Prayer, immediately beforehand. As the Lord's Prayer is recited by everyone at every Mass, it's not included in the Gospel readings on any Sunday. Matthew 6:14-15 is probably unknown to every Cradle Catholic unless they read and study the Gospels outside the Mass. You could go to Sunday Mass every Sunday of your life, and never hear Matthew 6:14-15 read, yet it's one of the most important verses in the entire Bible.

Reason #2: Confession misses our requirement to forgive others

If there's anything wrong with confession, it's that it ignores the need of the confessor to forgive others. I've never heard a priest ask in confession for me to search my heart for those times I've been hurt. Is there any unforgiveness in it? If so, I must forgive. If I don't forgive, then God will not forgive me. I've never heard that. If confession needs just one change, that would be it.

As a faith that relies upon the sacraments as the vehicle for God's Grace, forgiveness of others is, in retrospect, noticeably absent from Confession, at least in my experience, which is dated. The entire focus of the sacrament is in reconciling ourselves to God for sins we have committed. There isn't a focus on forgiving others, which is just as important. Forgiving others who've hurt us also reconciles us to God.

While the New Catechism (issued in the 1990s) describes our need to forgive others as "Astonishing" and "Daunting", where is the focus on forgiveness of others in the Church? You can find a few articles on the internet, but based on my experience and understanding, other than the verse in the Our Father recited at every Mass, that's it.

* * *

Insights on Forgiveness

I've been a student of forgiveness for a few years. In that time I've participated in forgiveness interventions for myself and others, helped facilitate forgiveness workshops, and researched various books, videos, articles, and other resources related to forgiveness. Listed below are what I believe to be important insights on forgiveness:

Key Insight: Some people find it easier to forgive than others, and the depth of each hurt varies. So the level of difficulty of forgiving a hurt can vary widely

This two-by-two matrix describes the dimensions that people and hurts fall into. *The Power of Forgiveness* documentary discussed earlier in this chapter describes recent scientific research that points to people falling into two categories: those that can naturally forgive easily and those that find it more difficult to forgive. Depending on your personality type and the depth of each hurt, you'll find it somewhere between no challenge to forgive and an extreme challenge to forgive a specific hurt.

Forgiveness Challenge 2 by 2 Matrix

Depth of Hurt:	Personality Type / Habit Formed:	
	Easily Forgiving	**Not Easily Forgiving**
HIGH	Moderate to Extreme	Extreme
LOW	None	Moderate

Key Insight: "Forgive and forget" is a myth and unrealistic for deep hurts

Little hurts can be forgotten but it's not possible to forget deep hurts and forgetting is not the point, forgiveness is the point.

Key Insight: If you haven't forgiven someone, you're the one who's harmed

Jesus' requirement of us to forgive others if we are to receive God's forgiveness (Matthew 6:14-15) may at first glance seem like a punishment. It's not. It's an invitation to the freedom and release that comes from forgiving others. I've seen this release first-hand and it's truly miraculous. Modern science is just now catching-up to the deep wisdom shared by Jesus in His *Sermon on the Mount* (Matthew 5-7) and other teachings two thousand years ago. There are a number of physiological benefits to forgiving, such as lower heart rate, reduced levels of stress, and other measurable benefits.

Key Insight: Forgiving Yourself Can Be Extremely Difficult

Some people harbor unforgiveness of themselves. Forgiving ourselves can be the most difficult type of forgiveness. Professor Everett Worthington, a university professor who teaches students about forgiveness, was able to forgive the murderer of his mother. He was also able to forgive himself for not doing more to prevent the suicide of his brother afterward. But, Professor Worthington found forgiving himself much more challenging than forgiving the murderer[29]. The Gospel verses that describe our requirement to forgive only speak to forgiving others. The verses don't seem to speak to forgiving ourselves. But, God's Grace is forgiveness of us. So if God has forgiven us through Jesus' suffering and death, then we know that God wants us to forgive ourselves, because he loves us. Forgiving ourselves can't be a requirement to receiving God's forgiveness, as that is not what the Bible verses describe. Why would God forgive you if he didn't want you also to forgive yourself? It wouldn't make any sense. If you struggle with forgiving yourself, **ask God for help**, and be open to his provision. I believe it's that simple. We must admit we can't do it on our own and rely upon God.

Key Insight: Resolving Anger with God Can Be Extremely Difficult

Some people are angry with God. Resolving anger with God can also be extremely difficult. Some people are angry at God for making them the way they are. Some people are angry at God for the loss of one or more loved ones. We know God is loving, and we know that God is merciful. So if someone has led a life that would lead to receiving Grace from God, and for whatever reason is angry with God, then it seems that God would understand. I believe that most if not all pain has an underlying reason that can be tied back to God's love. God's overall goal is for everyone's salvation and wants everyone to come to a knowledge of the truth (consider 1 Timothy 2: 3-4 in conjunction with 1 Thessalonians 5:18. Reconsider Jeremiah 29:11 in the context of eternity, not in the context of this life. Considering these three verses together points to the reason for pain and suffering, and should help you resolve your anger with God who has your long-term interests in mind). Sometimes God needs to introduce pain in peoples lives to draw them to Him. If we take a view of eternity, we should be thankful to God if he provides us the correction we need to change in order to enjoy salvation.

Key Insight: Test for Whether You've Forgiven #1: You Can Remember the Hurt and Don't Associate the Memory with Anger or Pain

Your memory of the hurt is a good indicator of whether you've forgiven the person who has hurt you or if you haven't. If you can remember the hurt and not have feelings of anger, not have a desire for revenge, then you've forgiven the person who hurt you. If, however, you become angry or have desires to retaliate, you haven't forgiven the person who's hurt you, and you must forgive them.

---

29 Professor Worthington has two "Do It Yourself" workbooks related to forgiveness that includes his personal testimony. Go to the bottom of the following webpage to download the workbooks: http://www.evworthington-forgiveness.com/diy-workbooks. Personally I think you can do a lot on your own to get started, but at some point you will need to ask God for help.

Key Insight: Test for Whether You've Forgiven #2: You Want[30] to Do Something Loving for the Person Who Has Hurt You, and You Do

A second test of whether you've forgiven someone is whether you've done something "loving" for them. Jesus on the cross asked God to forgive those who had tortured Him and were in the process of murdering Him. Implied in that request of God is Jesus' prior forgiveness of his torturers and murderers. Explicit in His request is an act of love. A deliberate kindness on Jesus' part to ask God to forgive those who tortured Him and were in the process of murdering Him.

Not only did Jesus want to do something loving for those who tortured Him and were in the process of murdering Him, he actually did. He put the idea into action. So did Stephen.[31] So did many Amish as described in the book *Amish Grace*. So did many of the families of those murdered in the Charleston, South Carolina Bible Study Massacre. *So can you.* "Perfect" or "Seal" your forgiveness with an act of kindness, and act of love.

Key Insight: Speed of Forgiveness Matters

Jesus led the way in forgiving others in "real time": Jesus forgave those who tortured and murdered Him as He was dying, providing an example to His followers. Stephen did the same, forgiving as he was being murdered by stoning. There are a number of anecdotes in the *Amish Grace* book of Amish forgiving in real time, forgiving immediately.

The murder by handgun of nine people in a Charleston, South Carolina Bible Study in 2015 saw many of the families of the victims explicitly forgiving the accused young man at his bail hearing, a hearing within a few days of the event (the bail hearing is viewable online). All of these examples of quick forgiveness were a choice. While all of those hurt experienced pain of the loss of a loved one, and forgiveness didn't remove the pain, all decided to avoid adding anger and bitterness to their pain. Most people forgive others after a period of time. As a result, there is a period in which anger and bitterness enters them and takes up residence. By forgiving immediately, anger and bitterness are never present in the person who forgives that quickly.

Key Insight: A Different Meaning to "77 times" (or in some translations "7 times 70")

When Peter asked Jesus if we need to forgive others who have hurt us as many as 7 times, Jesus' reply was that we need to forgive others "77 times" times (Matthew 18:21-22). This was Jesus' way of saying "unlimited". Most people, including myself, interpret Jesus' statement as forgiving multiple hurts by the same person. One woman in the Amish Grace book who lost a child in the Nickel Mines shooting provides an additional interpretation of Jesus' teaching: for really deep hurts, we may need to choose to forgive each day. This insight provides comfort to those who are hurt deeply and find they need to renew their choice to forgive repeatedly.

---

30 You may not "want" to do it as it is easier to do nothing, but you're at least "open to the idea" of doing something kind or loving for the person who has hurt you as you understand the benefits of "perfecting" your forgiveness.

31 Read Acts of the Apostles Chapter 7.

Working Through Unforgiveness of Past Hurts

While Jesus commanded us to forgive in the Lord's Prayer, and even reiterated the commandment immediately afterward (Matthew 6:14-15), He didn't provide details of how we should go about forgiving others. He did, however, model forgiveness. He showed us how to do it. Jesus forgave as he was being hurt, He forgave immediately. We should work to develop our ability to forgive as Jesus, Stephen, many Amish as described in the book *Amish Grace*, and many of the Charleston families forgave: immediately. But what about forgiveness of past hurts that have built up over time?

There are many approaches and methods for helping people forgive others for hurts that remain unforgiven. The next few pages describe a process that I've personally witnessed working more than once. It's wise to involve a Christian counselor or pastor or priest or deacon to help you work through pent-up unforgiveness.

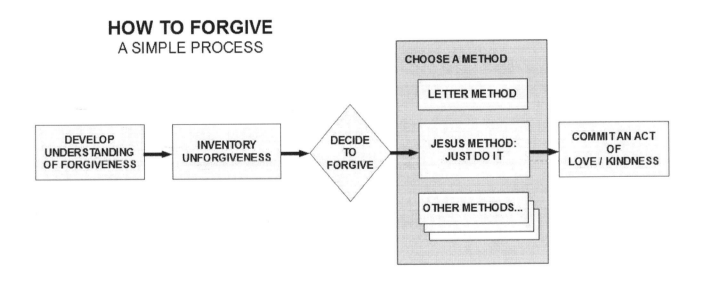

DEVELOP UNDERSTANDING OF FORGIVENESS – Use the resources listed in this chapter to develop your understanding of forgiveness. Followers of Jesus should be knowledgeable and even expert on the subject of forgiveness. As Brian Zahnd said in his book, "If Christianity isn't about forgiveness it isn't about anything at all." Learn all you can about forgiveness: study the teachings of Jesus, study what forgiveness is, study what forgiveness isn't, learn about methods and techniques of forgiving. Become a forgiveness expert in your family or parish or congregation or community.

INVENTORY UNFORGIVENESS – Use the template later in this chapter to develop a list of your hurts from the past and which of those hurts you've yet to forgive the one who's hurt you. Define the problem: how many people and how many hurts do you have to work through? Developing a complete list is the first step to forgiving all the hurts from your past.

DECIDE TO FORGIVE – You can be an expert on forgiveness but you still must decide to forgive. Even Professor Everett Worthington, a professor of Positive Psychology, a world expert on forgiveness, found it difficult to forgive himself for not doing more to prevent the death of his brother. Deciding to forgive yourself or deciding to forgive God may be the most difficult, but a decision to forgive is required in all cases. Look to Jesus, Stephen, the Amish, and the families of victims in the Charleston, South Carolina church shooting as role models: make a decision to forgive quickly. If you have unforgiveness from the past built up within you, the opportunity to forgive immediately after the hurt has passed, but now that you have your list of past unforgiven hurts, you have a second chance at immediate forgiveness. Once you've built your complete list, decide quickly to forgive everyone on the list.

CHOOSE A METHOD – Once you've made the decision to forgive, choose a method to facilitate your forgiveness. You may choose to "just do it", you may choose a method described in this chapter, or you may choose another method entirely. Follow through on your choice to forgive. I'm partial to the Letter Method because I've seen it work, but there are many techniques out there that may help you. Involve a Christian counselor or pastor or priest or deacon.

COMMIT AN ACT OF LOVE / KINDNESS – By committing an act of kindness, an act of love for those that you've forgiven, you are "perfecting" or "sealing" your gift of forgiveness. Your forgiveness is a gift that may be undeserved by the person who's hurt you. Your follow-up acts of love or kindness may also be undeserved. No matter. It's what Jesus instructs us to do and it's what Jesus modeled on the cross. Jesus' teachings are counter-intuitive and radical. They seem odd. But there's deep wisdom in His teachings. Take a chance, take a leap and follow Jesus' instructions, his commands. You'll be surprised by how well they work. The fact that the instructions came two thousand years ago before the discovery of electricity, before modern psychology, before the modern era, is amazing. The only possible explanation is that Jesus knows how we were designed and created.

* * *

How to Forgive Going Forward: Immediate Forgiveness

When I first read the anecdotes of the Amish forgiving immediately in the book *Amish Grace* I thought immediate forgiveness was interesting, but I never seriously considered immediate forgiveness as something I would do myself. In the process of writing this book I gave serious thought to Jesus' forgiveness on the cross and Stephen's forgiveness of those stoning him as he was being stoned to death. Then the Charleston Bible Study shooting happened. I had the chance to watch a video of the bail hearing for the accused and I was surprised to hear many of the families forgive the accused and even show acts of love and kindness toward the accused.

It was at that point that I thought immediate forgiveness was something that I wanted to try myself. You can count on those you live with to do something that will require your forgiveness with some regular frequency, as you spend so much time together. I decided to forgive Melissa immediately the next time she did something that hurt or offended me. As I've never forgiven someone immediately, I planned it out, similar to the activity later in this chapter.

> ℝ℞
>
> **Melissa's reaction [to immediate forgiveness] surprised me:**
>
> **she smiled...[immediate forgiveness] completely changed the situation.**
>
> ℝ℞

Not long after deciding to try out immediate forgiveness, Melissa said something to me that was said in an unkind way. I don't remember what it was, but it was in the morning and I said "I forgive you for speaking in a mean way to me". Melissa's reaction surprised me: she smiled. The stated forgiveness surprised Melissa so much that it completely changed the situation. Our conversation was pleasant and warm from that point onward. In addition to surprising Melissa, I think my immediate forgiveness forced Melissa to think of the situation from my perspective, forcing her out of her focus on "self" and into a mode of empathy. A week or so later I had the opportunity to extend immediate forgiveness again. It was morning and Melissa had not slept well. After she said something grumpy I told her "I forgive you for being grumpy towards me." Again, the unexpected and immediate forgiveness completely changed the dynamic. Immediately after forgiving Melissa there was an opportunity to do something kind and I acted on the opportunity, "perfecting" the forgiveness.

Intuitively we sense that there's a need to process what has happened before we can decide to forgive. Jesus, Stephen, the Amish and the families of the South Carolina Bible Study victims all demonstrate that we actually don't need time to decide to forgive, we can "just do it" even while the hurt is being committed. If we follow the example set by Jesus, Stephen, the Amish, and the Charleston families, we never allow hate, anger or revenge to reside in us. The hurt is, in a way, mitigated and the evil does not have a chance to carry on through retaliation. Going forward, start developing your ability to forgive immediately and see how it affects you and those around you. Once you've tested immediate forgiveness and seen how well it works, make it a habit.

Taking on BIG IDEA #2: Forgive Others – *No Exceptions*
A Simple Plan That Works

Putting BIG IDEA #2: Forgive Others – *No Exceptions* into practice starts with increasing your understanding of forgiveness: what it is, what it isn't, Jesus' instructions related to forgiveness. You may need to work through built up unforgiveness from the past, that would be the next major step after developing your understanding of forgiveness. Once you've cleaned out the unforgiveness from hurts from the past you can then focus on developing your ability to forgive others immediately. Activities and information that will help you complete the plan are in the pages following the plan.

Task	Description	Investment	Complete?
Read	**Read & Study the References to forgiveness in the Bible** [see Bible passages later in this chapter]	1 – 2 hours	☐
▶ DVD ▶ Watch	**Watch *The Power of Forgiveness* (DVD)** [see description of the documentary later in this chapter]	78 minutes $16* (DVD) (free on Amazon Prime)	☐
Read	**Read & Study *UNconditonal? The Call of Jesus to RADICAL Forgiveness* (book)** [see description of the book later in this chapter] Zahnd's book *Radical Forgiveness* seems to be the exact same book.	2 – 8 hours $15 new ($0.01-15 used)	☐
Read	**Read & Study *Amish Grace, How Forgiveness Transcended Tragedy* (book)** [see description of the book later in this chapter]	3 - 8 hours $15 new ($0.01-15 used)	☐
Activity	**Complete Activity 2.1: Inventory of Unforgiven People**	1 hour	☐
Decide	**Decide to forgive ALL who have hurt you** If necessary, take steps to stop from being hurt. Be safe. If you have unforgiveness from the past, the information in this chapter related to methods of forgiveness may help, and you can try use them, but seek out help from a pastor or priest or deacon or Christian counselor.	moment in time	☐

Task	Description	Investment	Complete?
Choose	**Choose a Method to Forgive, and Follow the Method** Read the descriptions of the "Letter Method" described later in this chapter. Find a pastor or priest or deacon or Christian counselor to help you work through the Letter Method for all past hurts that you have yet to forgive. Or make use of another method that the person who is helping you has used that works.	1 – 4 hours	☐
♥ **Love**	**Take action to "love one another as I have loved you"** Reinforce your forgiveness with one or more deliberate acts of kindness or love towards each of those you've forgiven. This extra step is modeled by Jesus on the cross, Stephen immediately before being stoned, various Amish in the book *Amish Grace*, and more recently by the families of the Charleston, South Carolina church shooting.	varies	☐
✍ **Activity**	**Complete Activity 2.2: Immediate Forgiveness Exercise**	varies	☐
Decide	**Decide to forgive all future hurts immediately** Be safe, take steps to protect yourself and those around you as needed, but develop your ability to forgive immediately.	moments in time	☐
			☐
			☐
			☐
PLAN TOTAL		10- 24 hours $0.00 – 32.00	☐

RESOURCE: The Bible (key forgiveness passages)

Use this page to track your progress in reading and studying the key forgiveness passages in the Bible. Check off each box as you read each passage (which are excerpted on the following pages).

Jesus' teachings provide the foundation for our understanding of forgiveness. Once I took the time to read and study these two passages, my understanding of forgiveness was completely different:

☐   **Jesus' Command to Forgive Others in his "Sermon on the Mount"** (Matthew 6: 5-15)

☐   **Jesus' "Parable of the Unforgiving Servant"** (Matthew 18: 21-35)

These five Bible passages reiterate the requirement for us to forgive others in all circumstances:

☐   **Jesus' Teachings on Forgiving Others** (Mark 11:25, Luke 6:37-38, Luke 11:1-4)

☐   **Paul's Teaching on Forgiving Others** (Colossians 3:13, Ephesians 4:31 – 5:2)

Jesus and Stephen demonstrate how we should forgive based on their own actions :

☐   **Jesus forgives His murderers** (Luke 23:33-34)

☐   **Stephen forgives those who are about to stone him to death** (Acts 7:54-60; 8:1)

Each of the passages is excerpted below. Four lines of the first passage and one of the other passages are excluded from the Sunday and Major Feast Lectionary, and will be new to Cradle Catholics whose only experience with the Bible are the verses read at Sunday Mass. Each is identified with the following notation:

*** NOT READ AT SUNDAY MASS ***

* * *

Jesus' "Sermon on the Mount" (Matthew 6: 5-15 (NRSV-CE), emphasis added)

When Jesus' disciples asked Him how to pray, he said they should pray privately and when they pray they should pray the "Lord's Prayer"as described below. After instructing the disciples how to pray, Jesus reiterates the importance of forgiveness, as described in the last four lines below:

> "And whenever you pray, do not be like the hypocrites; for they love to stand and pray in the synagogues and at the street corners, so that they may be seen by others. Truly I tell you, they have received their reward. But whenever you pray, go into your room and shut the door and pray to your Father in secret, and your Father who sees in secret will reward you.

> "When you are praying, do not heap up empty phrases as the Gentiles do; for they think that they will be heard because of their many words. Do not be like them, for your Father knows what you need before you ask him.

> "Pray then in this way:
>   Our Father in heaven,
>   hallowed be your name.
>   Your kingdom come.
>   Your will be done,
>   on earth as it is in heaven.
>   Give us this day our daily bread.
>   **And forgive us our debts,**
>   **as we also have forgiven our debtors.**
>   And do not bring us to the time of trial,
>   but rescue us from the evil one.

>   *** NOT READ AT SUNDAY MASS *** (the following four lines)
>   **"For if you forgive others their trespasses,**
>   **your heavenly Father will also forgive you;**
>   **but if you do not forgive others,**
>   **neither will your Father forgive your trespasses.**

Jesus clearly links God's forgiveness of us – God's Grace – with our forgiveness of others. In case we missed that connection, Jesus clearly describes our obligation to forgive others immediately after the Lord's Prayer, the last four lines above.

* * *

Jesus' "Parable of the Unforgiving Servant" (Matthew 18: 21-35 (NRSV-CE, emphasis added)
Melissa and I assisted Paul and Cyndi McCormick in their delivery of "Forgiveness Workshops" in 2014. Paul liked to include the following passage from Matthew in the workshop which he had read aloud to the workshop participants:

> Then Peter came and said to him, "Lord, if another member of the church sins against me, how often should I forgive? As many as seven times?" Jesus said to him, "Not seven times, but, I tell you, seventy-seven[32] times."

> "For this reason the kingdom of heaven may be compared to a king who wished to settle accounts with his slaves. When he began the reckoning, one who owed him ten thousand talents was brought to him; and as he could not pay, his lord ordered him to be sold, together with his wife and children and all his possessions, and payment to be made.

> "So the slave fell on his knees before him, saying, 'Have patience with me, and I will pay you everything. And out of pity for him, the lord of that slave released him and forgave him the debt.

> "But that same slave, as he went out, came upon one of his fellow slaves who owed him a hundred denarii; and seizing him by the throat he said, 'Pay what you owe.' Then his fellow slave fell down and pleaded with him, 'Have patience with me, and I will pay you.' But he refused; then he went and threw him into prison until he would pay the debt. "When his fellow slaves saw what had happened, they were greatly distressed, and they went and reported to their lord all that had taken place.

> "Then his lord summoned him and said to him, 'You wicked slave! I forgave you all that debt because you pleaded with me. Should you not have had mercy on your fellow slave, as I had mercy on you?' "And in anger his lord handed him over to be tortured until he would pay his entire debt. **So my heavenly Father will also do to every one of you, if you do not forgive your brother or sister from your heart.**

This parable is a graphic story that describes our obligation to forgive others. The "lord" and "king" in the parable is God. The wicked servant is both an encouragement that God's Grace can cover even the worst sinner, as well as a strong warning that we must forgive all others, without exception.

* * *

---

32 Some translations describe the number as "seventy times seven" or 490 times. Jesus' point is: without limit.

Jesus' Teachings on Forgiving ALL Others

Jesus instructs his followers to forgive others, no exceptions. We are required to forgive all others if we are to receive God's forgiveness for our sins. This requirement shows up in the Gospels at least three more times in addition to the passages above:

Mark 11:25 (NRSV-CE, emphasis added)

*** NOT READ AT SUNDAY MASS ***

"Whenever you stand praying, **forgive, if you have anything against anyone; so that your Father in heaven may also forgive you your trespasses.**"

Luke 6:37-38 (NRSV-CE, emphasis added)

"Do not judge, and you will not be judged; do not condemn, and you will not be condemned. **Forgive and you will be forgiven**; give and it will be given to you. A good measure, pressed down, shaken together, running over, will be put into your lap; for the measure you give will be the measure you get back."

Luke 11:1-4 (NRSV-CE, emphasis added)

He was praying in a certain place, and after he had finished, one of his disciples said to him, "Lord, teach us to pray as John taught his disciples." He said to them, "When you pray, say:

Father, hallowed be your name.

Your kingdom come.

Give us each day our daily bread.

And forgive us our sins,

for we ourselves forgive everyone indebted to us.

And do not bring us to the time of trial."

* * *

Paul's Teachings on Forgiving ALL Others

Paul also describes our requirement to forgive *all* others:

Colossians 3:13 (NRSV-CE, emphasis added)

Bear with one another and, if anyone has a complaint against another, **forgive each other; just as the Lord has forgiven you, so you must also forgive.**

Ephesians 4:31 – 5:2 (NRSV-CE, emphasis added)

Put away from you all bitterness and wrath and anger and wrangling and slander, together with all malice, and be kind to one another, tenderhearted, **forgiving one another, as God in Christ has forgiven you**. Therefore be imitators of God, as beloved children, and live in love, as Christ loved us and gave himself up for us, a fragrant offering and sacrifice to God.

* * *

Jesus forgives His murderers Luke 23:33-34 (NRSV-CE, emphasis added)
While on the cross Jesus asks God to forgive His murderers as they are in the process of murdering Him. Not after a few months or years, but as he was suffering. That's fast. But he didn't stop with simply forgiving his murderers, he followed up His forgiveness with an act of love, asking God to forgive those who were murdering Him:

> When they came to the place called The Skull, they crucified Jesus there with the criminals, one on his right and one on his left. Then Jesus said, **"Father, forgive them; for they do not know what they are doing."** And they cast lots to divide his clothing.

* * *

Stephen forgives those who are about to stone him to death Acts 7:54-60; 8:1 (NRSV-CE)
With Jesus as a role model, Stephen asks God to forgive those who are stoning him to death, including Saul, who would become the apostle Paul. Appreciate the speed of Stephen's forgiveness. As he was being stoned to death he forgave those throwing the stones. Also note that Stephen didn't stop with just forgiving those who were about to stone him. He also took the only action he could to love his murderers. Stephen asked God to forgive them. Stephen followed his forgiveness with an intentional act of kindness:

> [Stephen retraces Jewish history from Abraham through the crucifixion of Jesus in verses 1-53]

> When they heard these things, they became enraged and ground their teeth at Stephen. But filled with the Holy Spirit, he gazed into heaven and saw the glory of God and Jesus standing at the right hand of God. "Look," he said, "I see the heavens opened and the Son of Man standing at the right hand of God!" But they covered their ears, and with a loud shout all rushed together against him. Then they dragged him out of the city and began to stone him; and the witnesses laid their coats at the feet of a young man named Saul. While they were stoning Stephen, he prayed, "Lord Jesus, receive my spirit." **Then he knelt down and cried out in a loud voice, "Lord, do not hold this sin against them."** When he had said this he died. And Saul approved of their killing him.

* * *

RESOURCE: The Power of Forgiveness (DVD)
A film by Martin Doblmeier

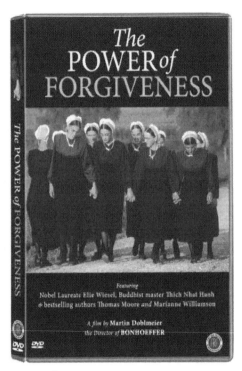

DVD Cover

The Power of Forgiveness video is the best documentary I've found to develop a better understanding of forgiveness. It's not without its faults (for example, I disagree with Thomas More's statement "don't let anyone talk you out of your desire not to forgive". I believe that is in direct conflict with Jesus' instructions and actions), but it does enlighten the viewer regarding cultural, scientific, and faith-based forgiveness concepts and insights.

Selected quotes from the video:

> "We tend to talk about justice far more often in every community that's been in torment...we rarely talk about forgiveness and mercy."
> (Bob Enright, University of Wisconsin professor teaching children in Ireland to forgive)

> "We have a biological process that's happening in our brain that rewards us for paying people back when they do something we didn't like...revenge excites pleasure pathways in the brain [similar to the effects of cravings for food and chocolate]...the soul seeks peace...but the brain seeks revenge" (Professor Everett Worthington)

> "the majority of faith traditions have always valued forgiveness...new scientific research reveals that: holding onto grudges is harmful...forgiveness is good for health"
> (Professor Everett Worthington)

> "I've practiced psychology for thirty years and I think most of the problems I see people struggle with have to deal with this issue [of forgiveness]." (Thomas More)

> "Forgiveness allows us to actually let go of the pain in the memory, and if we let go of the pain in the memory, we can have the memory, but it doesn't control us. When the memory controls us, we are then puppets of the past."
> (Alexandra Asseily, founder of the Garden of Forgiveness in Beirut)

I recommend *The Power of Forgiveness* to all Cradle Catholics. Through the video you can better appreciate the scientific research related to forgiveness as well as a few methods that are being used to facilitate forgiveness for individuals and for groups.

* * *

RESOURCE:
UNconditional?
The Call of Jesus to RADICAL FORGIVENESS
by Brian Zahnd

When I realized I needed to develop my understanding of forgiveness, I found *UNconditional* at the library and it was one of the most helpful books I found on the subject. It helped me appreciate forgiveness as central to Jesus' teachings. It helped me understand just how radical Jesus' teachings are. Six months later I checked the book out again and read it again. Eventually I purchased a copy. Then I bought more: it's one of a handful of books I give to others as a gift if I think they'll read it. This is one of the two best books I've found to help me understand Jesus' teachings on forgiveness outside the Bible (the other book is *Amish Grace*). Here are a few excerpts from the book:

Book Cover

"If Christianity is about anything, it is about forgiveness."
(page xix)

"...this book is about how Jesus forgives and how he calls us to imitate his practice of radical forgiveness. And radical is the appropriate word, because when it comes to the proclamation and practice of forgiveness, Jesus was the most radical innovator in history. When Jesus teaches on forgiveness, he pushes us to the extreme. Jesus seems to be indicating that our practice of forgiveness should be unconditional. But unconditional forgiveness is a tall order, and it requires some serious thought. Can we always forgive? Should we always forgive? If we always forgive, aren't we enabling evil? If we forgive unconditionally, aren't we sacrificing justice? These are some of the issues I attempt to explore in this book." (page xx)

"Make no mistake about it; this call to forgiveness is extreme. It's a call that transcends the bounds of what casually can be considered as reasonable. To follow Jesus as a disciple is to become a practitioner of radical forgiveness. Conventional forgiveness, easy forgiveness, reasonable forgiveness is what most rationally minded people are willing to engage in. Christ's followers are called to radical forgiveness, unreasonable forgiveness, reckless forgiveness, endless forgiveness, seemingly impossible forgiveness. The expectations regarding forgiveness that Jesus places upon his disciples are among the most demanding aspects of Christian discipleship, but these demands must not be ignored." (page 27)

"Forgiveness is not a feeling. Forgiveness is a choice to end the cycle of revenge and leave justice in the hands of God." (page 20)

"Forgiveness is not amnesia. You don't have to say you weren't wronged. Forgiveness is found in truth and not a lie. You can remember the wrong. It can be named and shamed as a sin. You don't have to abandon the hope of justice...you can leave justice in the hands of God." (page 84)

The book's chapters include:

  1: The Question of Forgiveness
  2: The Possibility of Forgiveness
  3: The Imitation of Christ
  4: No Future Without Forgiveness
  5: Forgiveness that Transcends Tragedy
  6: Forgiveness and Justice
  7: Killing the Hostility
  8: The Golden Rule and the Narrow Gate
  9: Beauty Will Save the World
  10: The Prince of Peace

I highly recommend *UNconditional* to all Cradle Catholics. The book is an easy read, yet its insights are powerful and life changing.

You may find *Unconditional* at your public library. It's available from retailers in hardcover and paperback format. I recommend the hardcover format as it will last longer and can be passed on to someone else in better condition. Amazon may have used copies of the book for sale at a discount. The book may be purchased in bulk from www.christianbook.com at a discount.

* * *

RESOURCE:
Amish Grace
How Forgiveness Transcended Tragedy
by Donald B. Kraybill, Steven M. Nolt, and David L. Weaver-Zercher

Amish Grace is another book I found helpful in understanding Jesus' command to forgive others without exception. It too is one of a handful of books that I give to others if I think they will read it. It's that valuable. Along with Brian Zahnd's *UNconditional*, it's one of the two best books I've found outside the Bible to develop an understanding of Jesus' teachings on forgiveness.

All Christians can learn from the Amish, who take their faith very seriously. I'm not talking about their obvious from a distance avoidance of modern technology (sometimes it has a certain appeal, other times not so much). I'm referring instead to the not so obvious from a distance approach of the Amish to forgiveness.

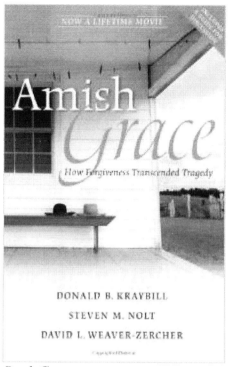

Book Cover

The Amish approach to forgiveness is powerful and establishes a clear role model for others to follow, in the same way that Jesus and Stephen provide clear role models for us in their actions of two thousand years ago. In their approach to forgiveness, the Amish practice what others merely preach, if they are even aware of Jesus' very specific, very radical teachings on forgiving others.

Here are a few excerpts from the book:

> *"If we don't forgive, we won't be forgiven"* - Amish Carpenter (p.85)

> One non-Amish observer remarked, "All the religions teach forgiveness, but the Amish are the only ones that do it." (page 86)

> "Another story that highlights the speed with which an Amish family extended forgiveness in the aftermath of tragedy came to us from the recipient of that gift of grace. In late October 1991, Aaron and Sarah Stoltzfus had enjoyed a happy day together. Married in an all-day wedding at her home the previous Tuesday, the couple had set out on their honeymoon. Unlike English couples, who might fly to a Caribbean island, the Stoltzfuses, following traditional Amish honeymoon custom, arranged to visit extended family for several weeks. During that time they received gifts, enjoyed a break from their work routines, and became better acquainted with their new in-laws. Now, five days after their wedding, they were returning home on Sunday afternoon after their first honeymoon visit.

That same day, seventeen-year-old Joel Kime came home from church, grabbed some lunch, and headed to a soccer game with his brother and two friends. Driving his family's old AMC Concorde station wagon, and eager to show off its power, he had already hit seventy miles an hour when he topped the crest of a hill on a narrow country road, only to find a buggy one hundred yards ahead. Unconcerned, he decided to "blow past those guys, because I thought it was so incredibly cool!" His daring turned into terror as the horse began to turn left into the passing lane. At his high speed, Kime had failed to see the buggy's turn signal. Newlywed Sarah died in the hospital that evening."
(page 72)

The authors continue by describing how the Amish groom and his family forgave Kime the next day, while just starting the process of grieving the loss of Sarah. They forgave immediately, not after weeks, or months, or years. Sarah's family and the larger Amish community extended acts of kindness and love toward Kime over the course of the following years. When Kime later married, the Amish came to the wedding and brought gifts, to Kime's astonishment. Kime was transformed by the experience.

The book's chapters include:

Part One
1: The Nickel Mines Amish
2: The Shooting
3: The Aftermath
4: The Surprise
5: The Reactions

Part Two
6: The Habit of Forgiveness
7: The Roots of Forgiveness
8: The Spirituality of Forgiveness
9: The Practice of Forgiveness

Part Three
10: Forgiveness at Nickel Mines
11: What About Shunning?
12: Grief, Providence, and Justice
13: Amish Grace and the Rest of Us

I highly recommend this book to all Cradle Catholics. *Amish Grace* will help you develop a better understanding of forgiveness as taught and modeled by Jesus. The description of the school shooting at the beginning of the book will bring a tear to your eye. The authors and the Amish interviewed in the book do a fantastic job of describing Jesus' teachings on forgiveness and provide clear and detailed examples of how they put His teachings into practice, and you can too. The "radical" and "unconditional" forgiveness Zahnd describes is demonstrated by the Amish.

Activity 2.1: List of Unforgiven People

How to complete this activity: Make a listing of those you have yet to forgive. Use the template below to develop your list. Think of all of the people in your past that have hurt you and each of the incidents of hurt (if you're still being hurt, you need to take action to protect yourself). Think of each person and how they hurt you. While you have not forgotten the hurt, is there still pain or anger associated with the hurt? If so, you have not forgiven the person, and add the person to your "List of Unforgiven People."

Be sure to consider family members, friends, acquaintances, yourself and God. Take a week to build your list. If you're married, have dinner with your spouse as Melissa and I did, to build the list. Think about the list for a week and then have dinner together and each build your list at dinner and discuss your lists. If you're not married, find a close friend or family member to have dinner with and build your lists. If you need more room, use a separate sheet of paper.

LIST OF UNFORGIVEN PEOPLE

Who	How Were You Hurt?	How Deeply?	When You Think of the Hurt, Do You Feel Pain?

Once you've listed all of the hurts in your life that you can remember, look at the last column. If you remember the hurt, but there are no painful feelings associated with the memory of the hurt, then you have most likely forgiven that person. However, if painful feelings are associated with the hurt, you haven't forgiven that person who hurt you.

Focus on the people on your list that you haven't forgiven, the people who have hurt you that you associate memory of the hurt with pain, or you are angry about the hurt, or you are seeking revenge for the hurt. You must now decide to forgive each of these people. You'll be a prisoner to the hurts of the past until you choose to forgive and actually forgive each person who's hurt you.

* * *

How to Forgive: The Letter Method

The following method can help you identify the hurts that you've yet to forgive and give you a process to actually forgive others. When done well, the method is powerful in working through hurts from the past. While you can attempt to work through the process on your own, it's designed to be done with the guidance of a pastor or priest or deacon or Christian counselor, so seek help to work through the process. Any of those people would be honored to help you work through your unforgiveness of past hurts into forgiveness going forward. They may have another method that they prefer. If so, use that. The method doesn't matter, all that matters is that you forgive:

Step 1: **Make an inventory of those you have yet to forgive**.
Use the template on the previous page to develop your list. Melissa and I went to dinner at a Mexican restaurant. It was a good choice. There was something about the level of noise, the comfort food, maybe it was the margarita, but the location worked well to develop our inventories of those we had yet to forgive. I recommend doing the same.

Step 2: **Write letters to each person on your list of those you have yet to forgive**.
Depending on how many letters you have to write, this make take an hour, a few days, or a couple weeks. Each person who has hurt you should be a separate letter, and each letter should have four parts:

Part 1: **Describe how you've been hurt and how it made you feel**:
"Dear [person who hurt you], " ...describe everything you always wanted to say to them, incident by incident, of how they hurt you. Use as much emotion as possible. It was emotional when they hurt you, bring it back up in the letter with the same emotion.

Part 2: **Forgive the person who hurt you**:
"And now, [person who hurt you], I forgive you. I forgive you for...[list out every incident of how the person hurt you]. Note: it's not necessary that you actually feel it, just that you mean it. This is what Jesus instructs his followers to do, so by doing it and meaning it, even if you don't feel like it, you are being obedient to God (who is having you do this for your own benefit).

Part 3: **Forgive yourself**:
"And now, [your name], I forgive you for carrying around all of this anger, this junk, this pain and

> ଈଔ
>
> # FORGIVENESS LETTER
>
> Dear [person who hurt you],
>
> 1: Describe the Hurt
>
> 2: Forgive the Person
>
> 3: Forgive Yourself
>
> 4: Ask God to Forgive You
>   for Not Forgiving
>
> ଈଔ

allowing it to garbage up my life, to negatively affect my life long after the initial hurt."

Part 4: Prayer:

"And now, Heavenly Father, I ask that you forgive me for not forgiving. In your Word, you commanded me to forgive, and until now, I haven't done it. Please restore the flow of your Grace to my life as I now forgive [person who hurt you]." Remember Matthew 6:14-15? If you don't forgive others, God doesn't forgive you. God gave us specific instructions for how we should live through Jesus' teachings, of which Matthew 6:14-15 is just one. By not following God's specific instructions for how we should live, we have disobeyed God.

Step 3: Read the letter to the "person"

Print out one copy of each letter. Be sure to destroy all other copies of the letter – paper or electronic – other than the one you print out. This will help you avoid going back to the letter to "stew" on the hurt. If you retain copies of the letter it could enable you to retain the hurt rather than let it go.

Set-up a chair in front of you and imagine that the person is sitting in front of you. Read the letter to the "person" in the chair and mean it. Read each of the letters you've written. If you've written a letter to yourself, read that last. Paul sat next to me as I did my reading out loud and, separately, Cyndi sat next to Melissa. I have sat behind others as they did their letter reading. The purpose of sitting next to or behind the person is to provide support and encouragement to the reader. You don't listen to what they're reading, but pray for them as they go through the process, and encourage them.

Step 4:Burn the Letters.

You read that right. Burn the letters. Once you've read all of the letters, go outside and burn them – on the grill or elsewhere – but burn the letters. This provides finality to the process. Burning the letters is an "event" you can look to that helps the process of forgiving. Don't be surprised if you laugh or smile. As the fire consumes the letter you will naturally be lifted up. Take a picture of the event. If more than one person has written forgiveness letters, have each person read their letter or letters separately, but burn the letters in a group and take pictures. Later, use the pictures to remember the event.

Step 5: Sleep on it and see how you feel the next day.

Melissa and I noticed a dramatic positive impact the next day. The positive impact of forgiving all others will favorably impact all of your relationships and have a ripple affect throughout your life and those around you. It all starts with the first step.

The "Letter Method" is based on the forgiveness counseling created by Paul & Cynthia Bixler McCormick, and Dill Pickle Love Ministries, in conjunction with Pastor Larry Russell. Melissa and I have helped facilitate forgiveness in Paul and Cyndi's forgiveness workshops and elsewhere. Seek out the support of a pastor or priest or deacon or Christian counselor to work through the process and forgive others, God and yourself for past hurts.

Activity 2.2: Immediate Forgiveness Exercise

How to Complete this Activity: Jesus, Stephen, many Amish in the book *Amish Grace*, and others have demonstrated an ability to forgive others immediately. Use the template below to plan out an act of immediate forgiveness and a follow-up act or acts of kindness or love (Be sure to take steps to protect yourself and others from those who are abusive, as appropriate).

Immediate Forgiveness Plan

Identify someone who you believe will likely require your forgiveness in the near future (a spouse, sibling, parent, etc.) for the minor hurts that we each inflict on one another in everyday life.

Name: _____

The next time they offend or hurt you, deliberately forgive them immediately. Avoid ever allowing yourself to be angry. Consider their actions from their perspective. Verbalize your forgiveness to the other person, describing what it is you are forgiving them for, as they are hurting you. Observe their reaction.

Plan a few potential simple acts of kindness or love that you could quickly perform right after or during your immediate forgiveness. List those here:

_____

_____

Immediate Forgiveness Reflection

Did you avoid all feelings of anger?

_____

What happened when you verbally forgave the person immediately?

_____

Once you've seen how it's possible to forgive immediately, to forgive in real-time, and once you've seen how immediate forgiveness changes the situation, you and the other person, work to increase your ability to forgive others immediately for all hurts.

BIG IDEA #3:
Read & Study the Bible,
But Immerse Yourself in the Gospels

Then Jesus was led by the Spirit into the wilderness to be tempted by the devil. After fasting forty days and forty nights, he was hungry. The tempter came to him and said, "If you are the Son of God, tell these stones to become bread."

Jesus answered, "It is written: 'Man shall not live on bread alone, but on **every word** that comes from the mouth of God.' "

Gospel of Matthew, Chapter 4, verses 1-4 (emphasis added)

* * *

"Few Catholics read the Bible. The church needs a massive Bible education program...**If you do not read and pray the scriptures, you are not an adult Christian**."

National Catholic Reporter, 2011[33]

---

33 article by Thomas Reese, "Hidden Exodus – Catholics Becoming Protestants, April 18, 2011, ncronline.org, emphasis added.

BIG IDEA #3: Read & Study the Bible, *But Immerse Yourself in the Gospels*

As a Cradle Catholic, I was both knowledgeable of Scripture and at the same time ignorant. Having participated in hundreds of Masses through the years, I heard many readings from both the Hebrew Bible and the New Testament. I heard the readings that are read at Mass multiple times. However, not until fairly recently in life, did I:

- read Jesus' "Sermon on the Mount", Matthew chapters 5 through 7 in its entirety in one sitting – not even once

- read any of the Gospels from beginning to end in one day or over the course of a few days – not even once

- watched any word-for-word performance of any of the Gospels

My experience until fairly recently was similar to that of most Cradle Catholics. I relied upon the Mass for my reading and study of the Bible. I was missing a lot. Anyone who relies upon the Mass as their only point of engagement with the Bible is missing a lot. If that's you, this chapter is intended to help you change. Changing your level of engagement with the Bible will definitely change your life.

Potential Objections to Reading & Studying the Bible

There are reasons why more Cradle Catholics don't read and study the Bible. Here are objections Cradle Catholics might have to reading and studying the Bible, and responses to each:

Objection #1: The Bible is HUGE. There's no way I could ever read and understand a book of that size!

Many people are intimidated by the Bible. It's a large book. My favorite study Bible, the Quest Study Bible is 1,800 pages in length. It's common to think of the Bible as a really long book that you start reading at the beginning, and then proceed to read from beginning to end like a really big novel. It's all in the Bible so it's all equally relevant to your transformation. Not so.

There are many Bible study plans that map out reading the entire Bible over the course of a year. How many people who start such a study actually complete it? Probably the same number of people who actually honor their own New Year's resolution: very few.

Maybe that's the reason so many people are fascinated with Creation, so many people engage in debate about creation: Genesis is the first book of the Bible. Maybe most people who set out to read and study the Bible never get past Genesis in their approach to reading the Bible like any other book?

While this fascination with creation is an interesting academic exercise, if you're not a theoretical physicist splitting apart atoms, you have more important things to understand and implement in your life, such as how you should:

- act in the here and now, day by day, moment by moment

- treat other people, treat your enemies

- pray

- store up treasure

- fast

- give to the needy

- settle disputes, forgive

- refrain from anger, worry, fear, and judging others

based on specific instructions given to us by Jesus that are in the Gospels. The instructions are not in Genesis. They are in the Gospels. The instructions, concepts, insights, and the like in the Gospels are *much* more important than understanding how the world and the universe began.

Other people seem to think the other end of the Bible, the book of Revelation, would be a good place to start. One young adult I had the chance to speak with was eager to start studying the Book of Revelation. I told him that I was still working on understanding Jesus' teachings in the Gospels and that I didn't ever think I would get to studying Revelation as there was so much in the four Gospels to understand and put into practice. I'm not sure if he made use of that guidance, but I stand by the advice.

People are fascinated by how the world will end, the "end times". Like the academic exercise of contemplating creation, this too is an interesting exercise, but if the world were to come to an end soon and you could actually make sense out of Revelation to point to when the end was going to happen, you would *still* need to read, study and immerse yourself in the Gospels in order to prepare yourself for the return of Jesus. Sort of like your Mom or Dad when you were young leaving specific instructions of things you need to understand and get done before they return, and instead of reading the instructions and getting things done you keep looking out the front window to see when their car is coming. Get away from the window, read the instructions, and do what the instructions tell you to do, and your Mom or Dad won't be disappointed when they get home to find that you didn't do what they specifically instructed you to do.

I wouldn't recommend starting with Revelation, just as I wouldn't recommend starting with Genesis. Revelation is at the end of the Bible and Genesis is the first book of the Bible. Both are in the Bible, all of which is the Word of God, so all the books are important. But some books of the Bible are more important than others. The Gospels – Matthew, Mark, Luke and John – are those more important books, and so the

Gospels are the best place to start. The Gospels make up only about 10% of the Bible, based on number of pages. Most Cradle Catholics have never read or watched a word-for-word DVD of even one of the Gospels in its entirety. Each of the four Gospels is somewhere between thirty and fifty pages in my favorite study Bible, the Quest Study Bible. In that Bible there are about 175 pages for the four Gospels within the 1,800 pages of that Bible (not including indexes, maps and the like at the end). In that Bible the Gospels are just under 10% of the entire Bible, not much longer than this book. So, while the Bible is huge, you should be focusing on reading, studying and immersing yourself in the four Gospels, and they are just a tenth of the entire Bible in length.

Objection #2: I went to Mass growing up. I heard the Bible read and explained at Mass.

A little more than half of the verses in the four Gospels are read at Sunday Mass. If your understanding of the Bible is limited to what is read at Sunday Mass, you've only heard a little more than half of the Gospels, about 58% of the Gospels according to Felix Just, S.J[34]. What you have heard read was read to you bit by bit over the course of many weeks, so your level of understanding of each of the Gospels is even less than if you read half a Gospel in a day or two.

Those are the major objections that a Cradle Catholic might have to reading and studying the Bible outside the Mass. If you're a Cradle Catholic like me, I hope I've convinced you that what you need to focus on reading in the Bible – the four Gospels – is a modest amount of reading. I hope that I've also convinced you that relying upon the Mass – if you even go to Mass – is not enough.

* * *

---

34 Checkout the Rev. Felix Just S.J.'s website: http://catholic-resources.org/Lectionary/

Why Your Grandparents Didn't Read and Study the Bible – But You Should

Four Factors that Have Limited Cradle Catholic Bible Reading and Study for 2,000 Years

Four important factors or trends have limited Bible reading and study among those born into the Catholic Church – Cradle Catholics like you and me – over the course of the last two thousand years. Each of the four factors has been a hurdle to widespread Scripture reading and study. All hurdles have been overcome, save the last one, which is in the process of being overcome. While these four factors have affected our grandparents and ancestors, they no longer prevent us from reading and studying the Bible. It's helpful to appreciate what prevented our ancestors from engaging the Bible outside the Mass, and how our situation is different:

Factor #1: Literacy: The ability to read and understand the Bible changed dramatically over time, especially over the past two hundred years. For most of the time since Jesus' resurrection the vast majority of the world was illiterate. Widespread literacy in current times encourages Bible reading and study. While the United States has had an impressive record of literacy since its founding, more than half the world was unable to read as recently as 1960. You can't read and study the Bible if you can't read. Only within the most recent fifty years or so has literacy been removed as an obstacle for most of the world.

LITERACY RATES: WORLD & USA
1820 to 2010

YEAR	WORLD %	USA %
2010	83	99
1960	42	98
1900	21	89
1870	19	80
1820	12	not avail.

Source[35]

This chart shows how the increased availability of Bibles drove literacy rates dramatically higher. With the widespread availability of the Bible, people now had a reason to learn to read, whatever their day job.

LITERACY RATES: BEFORE & AFTER FIRST PRINTED BIBLE

YEAR	NETH.%	Grt.Brit.%	Sweden%	Germany%	France %	Italy %
1750	85	54	48	38	29	23
1475	17	5	1	9	6	15
Growth %	400%	980%	4700%	322%	383%	53%

Source: (same as above)

---

35 Literacy statistics for both charts retrieved from http://ourworldindata.org/data/education-knowledge/literacy/ on March 9, 2015. Max Roser (2015) – 'Literacy'. Data sources: Burringh & Van Zanden (2009), Van Zanden et al (2014), OxLAD, Broadberry, & O'Rourke (2010), CIA and US National Center for Education Statistics.

Factor #2: Bible Availability: The Christian Bible in its various translations is generally considered the most published book of all time, with total production statistics ranging from 2.5 billion to 6 billion copies produced in the last 1600 years[36]. It wasn't as easy in the past to obtain a copy of the Bible in a language you can read as it is today. The first known English translation of the Gospels was completed in the 10th Century[37]. The Old English translation was inserted between the lines of Latin text of the *Lindisfarne Gospels*, which were created a few centuries earlier. There was only one copy of this English Bible translation within an illuminated Latin work of art. The cover of the Lindisfarne Gospels was encrusted with jewels, which were later stolen by invading Vikings.

Gutenberg revolutionized printing by producing copies of the Latin Vulgate Bible in the 1400s. Even though "as few as 185" copies of Gutenberg's Bible were ever produced, his production process was revolutionary.[38] Gutenberg Bibles were the first Bibles to be produced by machine, not by hand. Each copy sold for the equivalent of *three years* wages for a regular worker, and were sold to universities or wealthy families.[39] Before printing presses, books were laborious to make, expensive to purchase, and rare. It's estimated that at the time of Gutenberg's printing of the Bible, fewer than 30,000 books existed in all of Europe. In contrast, our county library in Colorado has about twenty times that number of books spread across seven locations in one county within one state.[40] Fifty years after Gutenberg's invention Europe contained an estimated 9 million books, mostly religious in subject.[41]

In 1525, William Tyndale completed an English translation of the entire New Testament. He attempted to have his translation printed in Cologne, Germany that same year, but his plans were thwarted. Tyndale was successful in having 6,000 copies printed in Worms, Germany the next year. Most of those copies were eventually confiscated by authorities and destroyed. Tyndale was arrested in 1535 and executed (better described as "murdered" or "martyred") by strangulation in 1536 and his body was later burned at the stake. Ironically, the King James Version of the Bible (KJV) was authorized a few years later by the King of England. The KJV was based primarily on Tyndale's translation.

From that point onward, translations of the Gospels, the rest of the New Testament, and the Old Testament were readily available and produced in volume.

The Douay-Rheims Bible of 1609 is generally regarded as the first complete English Translation of the Catholic Bible. Even using the date of the Douay-Rheims Bible which wasn't available for seventy years after Tyndale's translation, an English translation of the Bible has been available to English-speaking Catholics for about four hundred years. Even the most expensive study Bibles available today cost less

36 Retrieved from http://www.guinnessworldrecords.com/world-records/best-selling-book-of-non-fiction/ on April 20, 2015.
37 All historical references in this section retrieved from
    http://amazingbibletimeline.com/bible_questions/q2_history_english_bible/ on March 9, 2015.
38 Alistair McGrath, *In the Beginning: The Story of the King James Bible and How it Changed a Nation, a Language, and a Culture*, New York: Doubleday, 2001, page 15. Around 40 Gutenberg Bibles are known to still exist.
39 Ibid.
40 https://en.wikipedia.org/wiki/Douglas_County_Libraries. The Douglas County Library system serves about 300,000 people, has a staff of almost 300 people, and a circulation of about 8 million, which means each book or other collection item is checked out more than ten times each year.
41 Henry Tischler, *Introduction to Sociology*, page 354, further quoting Ramo (1996).

than a few hours' wages and are available immediately.

Factor #3: Catholic Church Policy: Church policy affected the level of encouragement parishoners were given to read and study the Bible. Before 1965 the Church discouraged everyone other than priests and academics from reading and studying the Bible as a matter of official policy. The Church was afraid that Scripture would be misunderstood or misinterpreted by anyone else. That helps to understand why your grandparents didn't read and study the Bible if they could read and it also helps to understand why the culture of the Church today is not one of Bible reading and study, the previous policy still influences the Church's culture.

That policy was reversed in 1965. *Dei Verbum*, a document that came out of Vatican II strongly encourages all people to read and study Scripture, and the recently updated Catechism of the Catholic Church echoes that encouragement. The Church has been solidly behind Bible reading and study for everyone since then, as official Church policy.

Factor #4: Catholic Culture: The only remaining obstacle to widespread Bible reading and study for Cradle Catholics is cultural inertia, the tendency of organizations to resist change. New traditions of group Bible reading and study are being formed, but much more is needed to complete the Church's transformation to one in which all Catholics actively read and study the Bible. Think of how different the Catholic Church and the world would be if all 1.1 billion Catholics read and studied the Bible, and immersed themselves in the Gospels. The Church – and the world – would be different indeed. Pope Francis is clearly a different sort of leader: he's humble, he's charitable, he's kind, he doesn't judge, he's forgiving, and he's loving. Where do you think he gets his direction for how he should live? It's simple. He's read and studied the teachings of Jesus that can be found in the Gospels and other books of the New Testament. He didn't limit himself to the readings at Sunday Mass.

So, what's keeping you from reading and studying the Bible? Your grandparents may not have been able to read. If they could, the quality of the Bibles and study Bibles available was low compared to what's available today. The Church, of which they were probably active members, discouraged Bible reading and study outside the Mass. None of that applies to you.

So, what's preventing you from reading and studying the Bible?

Answer: nothing.

How I missed BIG IDEA #3 as a Cradle Catholic
(and you may have too)

I missed BIG IDEA #3 for most of my life. Here's why:

Reason #1: I relied on the Bible readings at Mass as my only source of Bible reading and study

Most Catholics rely upon the mass as their primary means of reading and studying the Bible. For most of the almost 2,000 years since Jesus' ministry on Earth the vast majority of people didn't know how to read, or didn't have access to a Bible, so dedicating time at Mass to read the Bible was effective. Now, literacy rates everywhere are high. If you're able to read, which is virtually every adult on the planet, you can do more. Even if you go to Mass every Sunday, you would miss out on a lot. Significant amounts of the Gospels, the story of Jesus' time on Earth, the Good News of our salvation, specific instructions for how we should live our lives, are never read at Mass. *If you went to Sunday Mass every week of your life*, you would only hear read[42]:

56% of the Gospel of Matthew

61% of the Gospel of Mark

57% of the Gospel of Luke

60% of the Gospel of John

58% of the Four Gospels

The Gospels are the "Good News" of Jesus, the savior of the world. Are you satisfied with hearing a little more than half – 58% – of the Good News? You shouldn't be.

The other challenge Cradle Catholics have is that in relying on the Sunday Mass as our only source of hearing or reading the Gospels, we only hear a little bit of one of the Gospel's each week. It takes a year to hear a "complete" Gospel by going to Mass, but even then, you're only hearing somewhere between 56% and 61% of a Gospel. Imagine reading 58% of a book or watching 58% of a movie. Would it have the same impact? Would you understand it as well as reading the entire book or watching the entire movie?

What if you read a little more than half of a book over the course of one year, reading a page or two each weekend? Would you really understand the book? How would that be different than reading the entire book in a day or two?

What about a movie? What if you watched a little more than half of a movie, watching a short clip of the

---

42 Statistics provided by Rev. Felix Just, S.J. (Society of Jesus, a/k/a, " the Jesuits"), see http://catholic-resources.org/Lectionary/Statistics.htm

movie each weekend for a year? Would you really understand the movie? How would that be different than watching the entire movie in one day?

If you're relying on the readings at Mass for your understanding of the other books of the New Testament, the amount of each book that's read is even less. If you go to Mass every Sunday of your life and all major feasts and holy days, *by design* you'll only ever hear read...

16% of Acts of the Apostles

27% of Paul's Letter to the Romans

37% of Paul's First Letter to the Corinthians

no verses from 2 John

no verses from 3 John

no verses from the Book of Jude

How can this be? Here's how. The Bible readings at Mass are defined by the "Lectionary." The Lectionary sets out every first reading, second reading, responsorial psalm, and Gospel reading that's read at every Mass around the world. Before Vatican II, a meeting of Catholic Church leaders in the 1960s that made significant adjustments to the Church, the Lectionary was the same every year, the Lectionary had a one year cycle. So, before Vatican II even less of the Bible and even less of each Gospel was read at Sunday Mass. Before Vatican II, if you went to Mass every Sunday of your life, and if the Mass was your only regular source of Bible reading and study, you would only ever hear 22% of the four Gospels. Is it possible to really understand Jesus' teachings by hearing 22% of the Gospels? Would you be happy with 22% of the Good News? Vatican II's shift to a three-year Lectionary cycle resulted in a massive increase in the amount of the Gospels that Catholics heard at Sunday Mass: from 22% pre-Vatican II up to 58% afterward. But, even with that significant improvement, hearing 58% of the Gospels read over a three year period isn't enough.

Reason #2: I wasn't aware of great resources like Study Bibles, which make it much easier to read and study the Bible

It took working for a Bible publisher to realize that such a thing as a study Bible exists. I wouldn't read and study the Bible nearly as much if I just had a regular Bible. I have my Dad's Douay-Rheims Bible that was published in the 1950s and was available to me while young.[43] It's not very user friendly, not compared to a modern study Bible. There's not much in the way of support and guidance and the text is small and squashed together, making reading difficult. If it was the only Bible available I would use it, but I would definitely use a magnifying glass and strong reading light. Thankfully, I have access to more readable Bibles. Having Dad's Bible from the 1950s helps to appreciate how challenging Bible reading and study was in the not-so-distant past for Catholics.

---

43 Growing up we had Dad's Douay-Rheims Bible on the bookshelf along with a paperback Good News Bible with simple illustrations. Once in a while I read the Good News Bible, but never used the Douay-Rheims Bible.

Reason #3: I wasn't aware of great resources like word-for-word video performances of the Gospels, which make immersing yourself in the Gospels much easier

It took joining a weekly Bible study group to realize that high quality, word-for-word video of many of the Gospels are available on DVD. The video currently available for the Gospels of Mark, John, and Matthew are all excellent (see descriptions of each later in this chapter).

Early Christians benefited from hearing the Gospel of Mark performed by a master storyteller who memorized the Gospel, hearing that Gospel in about 90 minutes. That experience was lost for hundreds of years as the oral tradition was replaced by the written Gospel of Mark, only available to a select few. As Bibles became more available and literacy increased, more people read the Gospel of Mark but they were still missing out on the experience of the early Christians. Only within the past few years can we all experience the Gospel of Mark as the early Christians experienced that Gospel, as performed by Max McLean (see description of the DVD later in this chapter).

Reason #4: Bible Study groups were not in place in most of the Catholic parishes of which I was a member

Our current home church, Mountainview, has at least six weekly Bible study groups. I don't recall any Bible study groups at the Catholic parishes of which I've been a member.

Levels of Engaging God's Word

I relied on the Bible readings at Mass for my entire understanding of the Bible for most of my life. I was in "Step 1" in the chart below. We visited my sister, Mary, in Albuquerque and joined her for a service at Sagebrush Community Church. The Pastor's message that week was that we should all move up in the progression in the chart. He taught that we don't read and study the Bible for *information*, we read and study the Bible for *transformation*. Amen.

I added "WATCH The Word of God" to the Pastor's capability framework. Video performances of the Gospels and other books of the Bible are now available that supplement reading. Join a Bible study group to help you start reading and studying the Bible. Pick a few verses of the Gospels that resonate with you, memorize them, and see how they pop into your head at the appropriate time. John 6:12 "let nothing be wasted" which Jesus said after the miracle of feeding 5,000 in which there were leftovers is an example of a verse that I've memorized and I think of at times, reminding me not to waste resources.

LEVELS OF BIBLE ENGAGEMENT

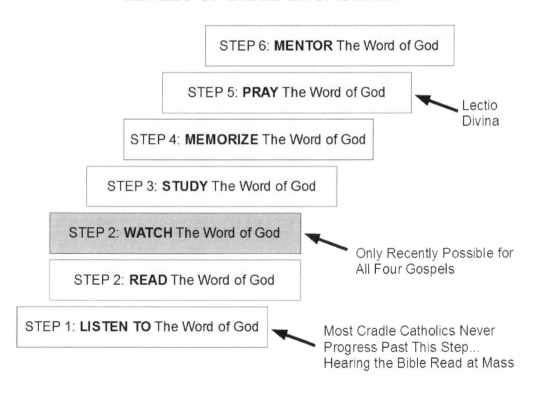

The ancient practice of "Lectio Divina" is a form of praying one or more verses of the Bible. There is good information out there on how to do it, including James Martin's *Jesuit Guide* book referenced earlier. The highest level of engagement is helping others develop their understanding of the Bible and application of it to their lives for their own transformation.

Most Cradle Catholics reading this book are at "Step 1". The activities, information and "Simple Plan" at the end of the chapter focus on helping you make it to Step 2 or Step 3.

Taking on BIG IDEA #3:
Read & Study the Bible, *But Immerse Yourself in the Gospels*
A Simple Plan That Works

Reading and studying the Bible, and immersing yourself in the Gospels is easier now than it's ever been since Jesus walked the earth. As a Cradle Catholic, your entire understanding of the Bible is probably from readings at Mass. It's time to step up. Here's a simple plan to help you immerse yourself in the Gospels.

The plan is based on the things I did that worked. The tasks are in an order that seems to make sense, but do them in any order that works for you. Check off tasks as you complete them in the rightmost column. Add new tasks using the blank rows at the end if you find something that helps you that isn't listed. The pages following the plan include information and activities designed to help you complete the plan.

Task	Description	Investment	Complete?
$ **Purchase**	**Purchase or Obtain a Study Bible that you will use** [see description later in this chapter] You can also use online Bible resources like www.biblegateway.com for reference.	0-60 minutes $0.00 – 40.00	☐
✍ **Activity**	**Complete Activity 3.1: Rate Your Current Level of Bible Reading & Study**	5 minutes	☐
✇ **Read**	**Read Jesus' "Sermon on the Mount": Gospel of Matthew, Chapters 5 through 7** Reading the "Sermon on the Mount" found in these three chapters of Matthew is like going to Mass and Jesus is giving the homily that Sunday. Jesus provides very specific instructions as to how we should act, think and interact with others. His instructions are revolutionary. You could spend some number of years working to align yourself with everything Jesus instructs us to do in these three chapters. Periodically come back to this reading and read it again.	1 hour	☐

Task	Description	Investment	Complete?
▶ **DVD** ▶ **Watch**	**Watch the "Sermon on the Mount" (youtube)** You can watch Jesus' "Sermon on the Mount" (chapters 5-7 in the Gospel of Matthew) in 21 minutes on youtube.	21 minutes free	☐
▶ **DVD** ▶ **Watch**	**Watch the "Sermon on the Mount" (youtube) multiple times** By watching the video multiple times, it will become a part of you.	free	☐☐☐☐☐
✍ **Activity**	**Complete Activity 3.2: Jesus' Instructions for Living** Become aware of Jesus' instructions and start to change to align the way you live with His specific instructions.	1 hour	☐
↻ **Read**	**Read The Gospel of Mark** Mark is believed to be the first Gospel written down, but was shared by word of mouth for years before it was written. Mark is the shortest of the Gospels in length, and many early Christians memorized the entire Gospel of Mark. You can read the entire Gospel of Mark in one sitting, a good place to start.	2 – 3 hours+	
▶ **DVD** ▶ **Watch**	**Watch *Mark's Gospel onstage with Max McLean* (DVD)** [see detailed description later in this chapter]	94 minutes about $14 (new)	☐
✍ **Activity**	**Complete Activity 3.3: Gospel of Mark Reflection & Notes**	5 minutes	☐
↻ **Read**	**Read *The Gospel of John*** The Gospel of John was probably the last Gospel written.	4 – 6 hours	☐
▶ **DVD** ▶ **Watch**	**Watch *The Gospel of John* (DVD)** [see description later in this chapter]	3 hours about $12 (new)	☐
✍ **Activity**	**Complete Activity 3.4: Gospel of John Reflection & Notes**	5 minutes	☐

Task	Description	Investment	Complete?
✒ Read	**Read** *The Gospel of Matthew*	4 – 6 hours	☐
✒ Read	**Read** *The Gospel of Luke*	4 – 6 hours	☐
▶ DVD ▶ Watch (Multiple Times)	**Immerse Yourself in the Gospel of Mark** by Watching *Mark's Gospel onstage with Max McLean* (DVD) Multiple Times (3 or 4+)	3 – 6+ hours (94 min. for each full viewing)	☐☐☐☐
▶ DVD ▶ Watch (Multiple Times)	**Immerse Yourself in the Gospel of John** by Watching *The Gospel of John* (DVD) Multiple Times (3 or 4+)	6 – 12+ hours (3 hours for each full viewing)	☐☐☐☐
♦ ♦ ♦ Join	**Join A Bible Study Group** [see description later in this chapter]	1 hour / week free	☐
▶ DVD ▶ Watch	**Watch** *The Passion of the Christ* **(DVD)** [see description later in this chapter]	2 hours about $5 (new)	☐
▶ DVD ▶ Watch	**Watch** *The Gospel According to Matthew* **(DVD)** [see description later in this chapter]	4 hours about $13 (new)	☐
✍ Group Activity (optional)	**Complete Activity 3.5: The "Other 42%" of the Good News Study (Group Activity)** This is an optional activity that is ideal for a group, If you're working through this book on your own you can skim through the verses to get a sense of what was excluded.	1 hour	☐
			☐
			☐
			☐
PLAN TOTAL		0- 40 hours $0.00 – 70.00	☐

RESOURCE: The Bible

A few bits of advice based on discussions with Cradle Catholics over time:

Which translation to use?

Many Cradle Catholics who decide to begin reading and studying the Bible wonder about which Bible translation they should use. I'm surprised by how many people who grew up Catholic are deeply concerned about translations of the Bible. If you are concerned, you can take comfort in this quote from the website www.catholic.com:

"What is the best translation of the Bible? The one you will actually read."

That statement was approved by the Catholic Church, based on the various official statements on the website. The statement is an encouragement for you to not worry, not be afraid when finding a Bible that you can read and study, if you care about the opinion of the Catholic Church. Then again, you may not particularly care what the Catholic Church's opinion is on translations of the Bible. The days of the various Christian denominations slanting translations toward their doctrinal views are in the past. Catholic scholars and non-Catholic scholars are working from the same original documents, and use the same techniques for translating from the originals into English.

Given the importance of the Bible, why not make use of multiple translations? The best online Bible resource I've seen is Bible Gateway (www.biblegateway.org). You can make use of more than thirty different translations of the Bible. You can also use the keyword search if you're interested in specific topics.

Jesus' View of the Bible

Jesus read the Hebrew Bible, the Old Testament, in synagogue (Luke 4: 14-30). Jesus was very aware of what he was doing or about to do that would fulfill what was foretold by prophets hundreds of years before he was born. Jesus explicitly stated that his teachings did not replace "the Law;" that is, the instructions given to Moses by God. Instead, Jesus described his teachings as an extension of the Law (Matthew 5: 17-20).

Clearly Jesus had read and studied the Bible as it existed in his day, and if you would like to answer Jesus' invitation to "follow me" that he extends to all of us, you'll need to follow His lead and read and study the Bible also. Thankfully, it has never been easier to do just that, as your abilities permit you to read the Bible and the Bible is readily available in a variety of formats.

* * *

RESOURCE: Study Bibles

Did you know that there's such a thing as a Study Bible? I didn't until I had the largest Bible Publisher in the world, Zondervan, as a client.

Obtaining a good Study Bible that you will actually use is a good first step in your project of reading and studying the Bible and immersing yourself in the Gospels. There are a variety of different study Bibles available. The best ones I've seen happen to be NIV and NLT translations, but the translation doesn't matter as much as how much you put it to use.

Here are some features to consider, in the order of importance from my point of view:

- Print Size (if you can't read the small print, it doesn't matter what the content is)

- Description of each Book (if you don't have a degree in Theology, these are very helpful)

- Articles, Questions & Answers (enables you to do some amount of studying on your own, whenever you have the time)

- Maps (helps you make sense of the places described)

- Indexes of Keywords (helps you undergo a personal study of anything of interest to you at a given time:: marriage, forgiveness, birth, death, etc.)

- Summary Charts (take advantage of the wisdom of Biblical scholars)

- Translation (there are a variety of translations available, but this is probably less relevant than the characteristics above, as you can always pick up a Bible in a given translation, but not all of the translations have usable Study Bibles)

* * *

Recommended Study Bibles: I didn't realize there was such a thing as a Study Bible until I worked on a project in Grand Rapids, Michigan for Zondervan Publishing, one of the largest Bible publishers in the world. Study Bibles are an incredible resource that can make reading and studying the Bible much more productive. The following study Bibles are ones I've found to be especially useful. There are many good study Bibles out there, so make your own choice, but consider these if you aren't sure what you're looking for. Study Bibles can seem expensive and vary widely in what's provided in the "study" part of the book. You may find it helpful to go to a Christian retailer (Family Christian Stores with about 250 stores across the US, Lifeway with about 180 stores across the US), Barnes & Noble, or an independent bookstore to see the differences. If you do, purchase the Study Bible where you find the one that meets your needs. If you know what you're looking for you may be able to purchase a Study Bible used on Amazon.com for a modest price:

Bible Cover

Quest Study Bible (Zondervan Publishing, hardcover, used) My favorite study Bible, and the one I gift to others most often is the Quest Study Bible. I prefer the older edition (with the Tree on the cover) as it's more readable than the current edition, at least for my aging eyes. You may prefer the newer edition (about $28 on Amazon), especially if the publisher makes the print more like the older version (larger, bolder print). I buy copies used on Amazon (good condition or better) for anywhere from $2 to $10 each plus $3.99 to ship. As you read the Bible, questions naturally come to mind. The Quest Study Bible has many of the questions that would occur to you in the margins with answers written by scholars. There are also questions that you or I wouldn't come up with but we would agree are good questions right there in the margins as well, along with answers written by a team of scholars. The Quest Study Bible enables you to have a personal Bible Study, facilitated by a group of scholars, on a long plane ride, at two in the morning, at the park. Anywhere, really.

Bible Cover

Life Application Study Bible (hardcover) (Tyndale Publishing, hardcover, new or used) After the Quest Study Bible, The Life Application Study Bible is my next favorite study Bible. It has more of a focus on applying the teachings in the Bible to life than other Study Bibles. I find the text easy to read. There's also a large print version you should check out if text size is a challenge. If I couldn't find an older version of the Quest Study Bible, I would choose this Bible. While you can find copies of this Study Bible used on Amazon for about $20 including shipping, that's not much of a discount from the price of a new one: about $28 new plus shipping, so buying new is probably the better choice. If you do purchase this Study Bible used, be sure to purchase "Good" or better condition, as "Acceptable" never seems to be worthwhile.

Activity 3.1: Rate Your Current Level of Bible Reading & Study

How to Complete this Activity: Look at the "Levels of Bible Engagement" chart on the previous page. Identify which "STEP" best describes your current level of engagement with the Bible. Identify the next "STEP" higher on the chart and specific actions you can take to move up to that next level. Put into practice the actions.

Current Level of Bible Engagement
STEP _____ _____

Next Level of Bible Engagement
STEP _____ _____

Specific Actions to Move to the Next Level
1. _____
2. _____
3. _____

Activity 3.2: Jesus' Instructions for Living

How to Complete this Activity: Read Jesus' sermon, the "Sermon on the Mount," in the Gospel of Matthew, Chapters 5 through 7. If you haven't found a good Bible or Study Bible yet, use www.biblegateway.com or another online Bible). Identify Jesus' instructions for living. Record in your own words Jesus' instructions. The following pages have been formatted to point you to the verses with instructions. Use the blank rows at the end for any additional instructions you find. Identify which instructions are a priority for you, instructions that require you to change in order to align your actions with them. Strive to follow Jesus' instructions and change as needed.

Chapter/Verse	Jesus' Instruction for Us	Priority?
Matthew 5: 16		☐
Matthew 5: 22		☐
Matthew 5: 23-24		☐
Matthew 5: 25-26		☐
Matthew 5: 28		☐
Matthew 5: 32		☐
Matthew 5: 34-37		☐
Matthew 5: 39		☐
Matthew 5: 40		☐
Matthew 5: 41		☐
Matthew 5: 42		☐
Matthew 5: 44-48		☐
Matthew 6: 1-4		☐
Matthew 6: 6		☐

Chapter/Verse	Jesus' Instruction for Us	Priority?
Matthew 6: 7-8		☐
Matthew 6: 9-13		☐
Matthew 6: 14-15		☐
Matthew 6: 16-18		☐
Matthew 6: 19-21		☐
Matthew 6: 22-23		☐
Matthew 6: 24		☐
Matthew 6: 25-34		☐
Matthew 7: 1-5		☐
Matthew 7: 6		☐
Matthew 7: 7-11		☐
Matthew 7: 12		☐
Matthew 7: 13-14		☐
Matthew 7: 15-20		☐
Matthew 7: 21		☐
Matthew 7: 24-27		☐
Other: _____		☐
Other: _____		☐
Other: _____		☐

RESOURCE:
Mark's Gospel on stage with Max McLean (DVD, 2012)

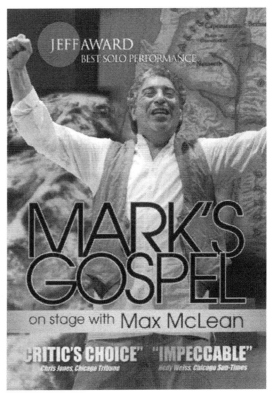

Max McLean's award winning Chicago Theater District word-for-word solo performance of the Gospel of Mark is a powerful and convenient way to take in the entire Gospel of Mark in one sitting.

As you watch Max's performance, notice how you pick up on some things in watching the DVD that you don't pick up reading the Gospel: humor, sadness, joy.

Many Cradle Catholics have never read a complete Gospel. Fewer still have taken in a performance of a Gospel. With this DVD you can see the entire Gospel of Mark performed by a master storyteller in 94 minutes.

In watching Max perform the Gospel, you're having much the same experience as the early Christians (except in English instead of Greek, or Aramaic, or some other language you don't understand).

Max's preparation shows. As a result of his study of the Gospel and precise performance, you'll have a much deeper understanding of the Gospel of Mark than if you simply read the Gospel.

The handful of special effects are all simple, appropriate and well done: maps projected behind Max help to understand Jesus' movement across Israel as described by the Gospel, and a few simple stage effects (lightning, thunder, changes in lighting) add to the impact of the performance.

Mark is the shortest of the Gospels, was likely written first, and was likely performed by master storytellers in much the same way as Max performs it: with passion.

The DVD makes it easy to immerse yourself in Mark's Gospel, simply watch it a few times. Consider inviting friends over to watch the DVD. The DVD does not currently have subtitles but the production company is considering adding them. If they do become available, use them for a more productive viewing of the performance.

Own a copy of this DVD and watch it more than once.

Consider giving this DVD as a gift to those you think will watch it.

* * *

Activity 3.3: Gospel of Mark DVD Reflection & Notes

How to Complete this Activity: Watch the *Mark's Gospel onstage with Max McLean* DVD, which should take about 94 minutes. Use the prompts below to reflect on the performance and take notes.

Gospel of Mark DVD Reflection
What did you learn in watching the performance?
What are your favorite parts?
Did you find anything humorous? sad? surprising?
Will you do anything differently having watched the performance?
What questions arise in your mind having watched the performance?
Will you recommend or gift this DVD to others? Why?

Gospel of Mark DVD Notes

RESOURCE:
The Gospel of John (DVD, 2004)

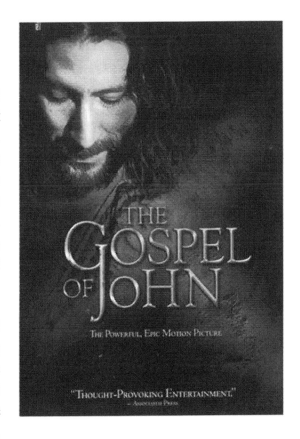

This presentation of the Gospel of John has more of a feel of a movie than Max McLean's performance of Mark, yet it too is a word-for-word presentation of an entire Gospel. Christopher Plummer (Captain Von Trapp in the classic "The Sound of Music" film) narrates the film. Henry Ian Cusick, a Scottish-Peruvian actor with Shakespearean stage acting experience plays a very compelling Jesus. Henry is clearly well prepared for the part and is clearly a highly gifted actor. The entire production is carefully crafted and high quality.

The script is the Good News translation, which is a good choice for a movie-like performance as it flows well. Filming was done in Canada and Spain. The German Catholic Church has been in the news recently for extravagant spending on remodeling fixtures[44]. The German Catholic church also apparently provided funding for this production, and for that I'm thankful, as it's the best video production of any of the Gospels I've ever seen. The film cost $16 million to produce, which is high for a film of this type. After grossing only $4 million at the box office the production company declared bankruptcy and Buena Vista (Disney) picked up the distribution rights. The DVD is available through Amazon.

I recommend turning on subtitles to hear what's being said, read what's being said, and see what's being performed, all at the same time. You will pick up more with subtitles turned on. The entire Gospel of John is presented in about 3 hours. Watch it all in one sitting or split up your viewing across two days. Consider inviting friends over to watch it and share a meal. This DVD also makes it easy to immerse yourself in the Gospels: simply watch the entire DVD multiple times. Once you've watched it four or five times you'll be able to recall key passages from memory. It really will change you.

Own a copy of this DVD and watch it more than once.

Consider giving this DVD as a gift to those you think will watch it. One of the versions of the DVD sold has two DVDs in a set: one DVD is the full three hour performance, and the second DVD contains two hours of "highlights" and information about the making of the film. I buy used copies of the 2 DVD set from Amazon and pull out the second DVD and stick it in a CD case and put it in my backpack. If I see someone reading the Bible in public, I offer them the DVD with the highlights and tell them they can buy the full three hour version in Amazon for about $12.

---

44 According to a Forbes magazine article, one Bishop of Germany spent $40 million renovating his official residence. As an example (*Forbes*, October 24, 2013, "Vatican Suspends 'Bishop of Bling' Over $40 million Home Renovation")

Activity 3.4: Gospel of John DVD Reflection & Notes

How to Complete this Activity: Watch the *Gospel of John* DVD, which should take about 3 hours. Use the prompts below to reflect on the performance and take notes.

Gospel of John DVD Reflection

What did you learn in watching the performance?

What are your favorite parts?

Did you find anything humorous? sad? surprising?

Will you do anything differently having watched the performance?

What questions arise in your mind having watched the performance?

Will you recommend or gift this DVD to others? Why?

Gospel of John DVD Notes

RESOURCE: A Weekly Bible Study

I've been in a Bible Study group that meets at our non-denominational church, Mountainview, at 6:00 AM Friday mornings for a few years now. I miss some of the meetings when the semester heats up and I find myself tutoring later in the evenings as students prepare for final exams, but I am a regular member of the group.

> ℘℘
> **Active participation**
> **in a weekly Bible Study group**
> **is critical to your**
> **growth and development.**
> ℘℘

The Friday morning 6:00 AM Bible study group has had a significant impact on my development. If I wasn't in the study group, I wouldn't have realized Max McLean's word-for-word performance of the Gospel of Mark even existed. Our Friday morning group studied the Gospel of Mark using that DVD, one chapter each week. I liked that DVD so much that I searched out all of the word-for-word performances of the Gospels and as a result found the other Gospel DVDs, John being the best, and Matthew worth watching as well. Both are described in more detail later in this chapter.

In the last couple years we've also studied the Book of Daniel, Paul's First Letter to the Colossians, the Gospel of John, the Book of Revelation, and presentations by Tony Campolo, N.T. Wright, and others given at the "Simply Jesus Gathering" Conference that were recorded on DVD. We just began a study of N.T. Wright's *Surprised by Scripture*. Some of the studies were life changing, some I would have avoided if it were up to me but I benefited from them nonetheless.

The Friday morning group is a mix of men. About half are members of Mountainview where the study is held, and half are members of other churches. One person leads the group, but assigns a different person to lead the study each week, typically a chapter in the book of the Bible that's under study. The week you're assigned to lead the study you're also responsible for bringing something to eat. We brew a pot of coffee. For some of the studies of books of the Bible we use study guides from the internet or purchase copies of a study guide book, but we don't really need them.

Active participation in a weekly Bible Study group is critical to your growth and development, just as it was and is to mine. Search out the Bible Study groups in your area. Find one that fits your schedule and make it a weekly habit. I think meeting weekly is the ideal frequency. Less frequent meetings would lack momentum, not making much progress. Bible Study groups are like churches and congregations: there's a lot of diversity, so check out what's available in your area, try each out, and pick the one that best fits your schedule and growth needs. Realize that you'll be welcome in any group, even if you aren't a member of that congregation, so be open to all options in your area and find the one that's best for you.

RESOURCE:
The Passion of the Christ (DVD, 2010)
Directed by Mel Gibson

While *The Passion of the Christ* is not a word-for-word performance of one of the Gospels, and while it does take some artistic license with a few details, it's clearly inspired. I don't believe anyone could watch the film and not be moved to tears.

I recommend watching the film to better understand the suffering Jesus went through in the twelve hours leading up to his death for our benefit. The film runs a little more than two hours and ends with Jesus leaving the tomb, with nail holes visible in his hands, a fascinating special effect. The actors speak ancient languages (Aramaic, Hebrew and Latin), with subtitles available in English and Spanish. You can purchase the DVD from Amazon for $5, which is probably close to the cost of producing and distributing the DVD.

RESOURCE:
The Gospel According to Matthew (DVD, 2010)

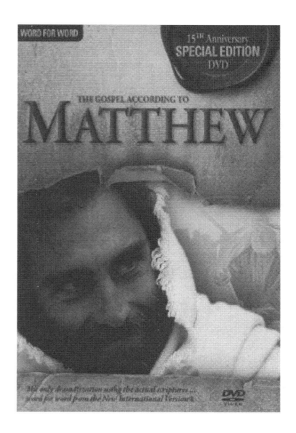

This word-for-word performance of Matthew is worth watching. It runs four hours which isn't surprising as the Gospel of Matthew is longer than Mark and longer than John. The Sermon on the Mount (Chapters 5 through 7) is a high point, although it would be better without the flashbacks to Matthew narrating.

Students at a private Christian school who I've shown the film to were impressed with Bruce Marchiano's portrayal of Jesus. Just watching a Gospel film was a first for most students and Jesus seemed more real to them after watching the film than before.

The DVD is available from Amazon for about $12 and the performance is loaded onto two DVDs.

Activity 3.5: The "Other 42%" of the Good News Study (Group Activity)

Even if you go to Sunday Mass every week of your life (which you probably aren't doing now but may have at some point in your life) you'll only ever hear read about 58% of the Gospels, a little more than half the "Good News." The verses listed on the following four pages are those parts of the Gospels that you won't hear read at Sunday Mass, the "other 42%" of the Good News. The list of excluded verses was derived from the Lectionary statistics provided by the Rev. Felix Just, S. J., a Jesuit priest[45].

While reading, watching, and studying *complete* Gospels is definitely more beneficial to your development, this can be an interesting exercise for Cradle Catholics. As you go through the activity, keep in mind that the current Lectionary was a big improvement from the Lectionary before Vatican II in the 1960s in which only about 22% of the Gospels were read at Sunday Mass. The right answer, of course, is to read and study *complete* Gospels outside the Mass in a much shorter period of time. You should be able to read a complete Gospel in one or two days. You can watch a complete word-for-word performance of a Gospel in 1.5 to 4 hours, depending on which Gospel you're watching.

How to Complete this Activity: This is an activity that's best done by a group of people working in four teams, one for each of the Gospels (if you're working through the 5 BIG IDEAS on your own, skip this activity). Divide your group into four teams and assign one of the Gospels to each team. Each team should review the excluded verses listed on the following pages for their assigned Gospel and make notes of what is interesting or surprising in the excluded verses. After twenty or thirty minutes, each group should share what they've learned, their impression of what is missed by Cradle Catholics who never hear or read the excluded verses. You can take notes in the area below of your overall impressions.

Review Summary
Matthew:
Mark:
Luke:
John:

---

45 see http://catholic-resources.org/Lectionary/

Gospel of Matthew: "The Other 42% of the Good News"

Excluded Verses	Key Messages
Matthew 2: 16-18	
Matthew 4: 24-25	
Matthew 6: 1-23	
Matthew 7: 1-20, 28-29	
Matthew 8: 1-34 (entire chapter)	
Matthew 9: 1-8, 14-35	
Matthew 10: 9-25, 34-36	
Matthew 11: 1, 12-24	
Matthew 12: 1-50 (entire chapter)	
Matthew 13: 53-58	
Matthew 14: 1-12, 34-36	
Matthew 15: 1-20, 29-39	
Matthew 16: 1-12, 28	
Matthew 17: 10-27	
Matthew 18: 1-14	
Matthew 19: 1-30 (entire chapter)	
Matthew 20: 17-34	
Matthew 21: 12-27, 44-45	
Matthew 22: 22-33, 41-46	
Matthew 23: 13-39	
Matthew 24: 1-36, 45-51	
Matthew 25 (none)	n/a
Matthew 26: 1-13	
Matthew 27: (none)	n/a
Matthew 28: 11-15	

* * *

Gospel of Mark: "The Other 42% of the Good News"

Excluded Verses	Key Messages
Mark 1 (none)	n/a
Mark 2: 13-17	
Mark 3: 7-19	
Mark 4: 1-25	
Mark 5: 1-20	
Mark 6: 14-29, 35-56	
Mark 7: 9-13, 16-20, 24-30	
Mark 8: 1-26, 36-38	
Mark 9: 1, 11-29, 44, 46, 49-50	
Mark 10: 1, 31-34	
Mark 11: 11-33	
Mark 12: 1-27, 35-37	
Mark 13: 1-23	
Mark 14: (none)	n/a
Mark 15: (none)	n/a
Mark 16: 8-14	

* * *

Gospel of Luke: "The Other 42% of the Good News"

Excluded Verses	Key Messages
Luke 1: 5-25, 51-52, 55-80	
Luke 2: (none)	n/a
Luke 3: 7-9, 19-20, 23-37	
Luke 4: 31-44	
Luke 5: 12-39	
Luke 6: 1-16, 18-19, 46-49	
Luke 7: 18-35	
Luke 8: 4-56	
Luke 9: 1-10, 25-27, 37-50	
Luke 10: 13-16, 21-24	
Luke 11: 14-54	
Luke 12: 1-12, 22-31, 54-59	
Luke 13: 10-21, 31-35	
Luke 14: 2-6, 15-24, 34	
Luke 15: (none)	n/a
Luke 16: 14-18	
Luke 17: 1-4, 20-37	
Luke 18: 15-43	
Luke 19: 11-27, 41-48	
Luke 20: 1-26, 39-47	
Luke 21: 1-4, 20-24, 29-33, 37-38	
Luke 22: 1-13	
Luke 23: (none)	n/a
Luke 24: (none)	n/a

* * *

Gospel of John: "The Other 42% of the Good News"

Excluded Verses	Key Messages
John 1: 43-51	
John 2: 12	
John 3: 1-13, 22-36	
John 4: 1-4, 43-54	
John 5: 1-47 (entire chapter)	
John 6: 16-23, 36-40, 59, 70-71	
John 7: 1-36, 40-53	
John 8: 12-59	
John 9: (none)	n/a
John 10: 19-26, 31-42	
John 11: 46-57	
John 12: 1-11, 17-19, 34-50	
John 13: 16-30, 36-38	
John 14: 13-14, 22, 30-31	
John 15: 18-25	
John 16: 1-11, 16-33	
John 17: (none)	n/a
John 18: (none)	n/a
John 19: (none)	n/a
John 20: 10-18	
John 21: 20-25	

* * *

BIG IDEA #4:
Find a Peace You've Never Known

"Have no anxiety at all, but in everything, by prayer and petition, with thanksgiving, make your requests known to God. Then the peace of God that surpasses all understanding will guard your hearts and minds in Christ Jesus"

Philippians 4:6-7, NAB-RE, emphasis added

BIG IDEA #4: Find a Peace You've Never Known

How many people truly understand the meaning of "peace," as Jesus used the word? Do you? Peace is a word that's common in the Catholic Church, so as a Cradle Catholic you're familiar with the word. But do you understand what it truly means?

Until recently, I didn't understand and appreciate the meaning of the word, "peace" as described by:

- the prophet Isaiah: about *700 years before* Jesus' birth, Isaiah predicted the coming Messiah, or Savior of the World (Jesus), and gave Jesus a variety of titles, including the "Prince of Peace",

- Jesus speaking of peace as a state of being in His teachings

- the Apostle Paul: Paul uses the word "peace" in virtually all of his letters found in the New Testament, wishing it for those to which he was writing. Paul also describes peace as one of the "fruits of the Spirit", or outcomes of "living by the Spirit."[46]

My understanding of the word "peace" for most of my life was along the lines of an "end to war." While the word does mean the end of hostilities between nations, it also has a more personal meaning – personally experiencing a deep sense of well being that can only come from a healthy relationship with God, healthy relationships with all other people, and a healthy relationship with yourself.

* * *

Getting to Peace

So, how do we experience this deep sense of peace that Isaiah, Jesus, Paul and others spoke or wrote about and that Catholics wish each other at every Mass? It's not something we can pursue directly. I believe a deep sense of peace can be found by focusing on BIG IDEA numbers 1 and 2, accepting God's Grace, or forgiveness of us, forgiving all others who have hurt us, and then by following Jesus' teachings, which are learned by immersing yourself in the Gospels (BIG IDEA #3). Jesus doesn't give peace like the world gives (John 14:27): the peace of Jesus is eternal, the peace the world gives is fleeting and temporary, if it even gives peace. Here's how Jesus leads to peace:

> **Peace by way of Accepting God's Grace**: By dying on the cross for our sins, Jesus enables God's forgiveness of our sins. Once someone confronts their own sin, they could fall into despair after realizing what they had done. Jesus' sacrifice enables each of us to rise above our sins, out of the "valley of death". You can't find peace if you stew on the mistakes of the past.

---

46 Paul described the "fruits of the spirit" in Galatians 5: 22-23 as: love, joy, peace, patience, kindness, goodness, faithfulness, gentleness and self-control.

Peace by way of the Forgiveness of Others: By commanding us to forgive others in all cases, God frees us from holding anger inside. It's not obvious that the personal requirement to forgive others results in us being less angry. Anyone who's resisted forgiving one or more people and then decided to forgive, and actually did forgive, knows the release that's felt, a massive internal shift away from anger toward peace.

Peace by Way of Following Jesus' Instructions, But Especially the Instructions of Don't Worry, Don't Be Afraid, and Serve Others: If you're working through BIG IDEA #3, you're immersing yourself in the Gospels. Once you decide to rearrange your life to live out what you read (or see and hear on DVD) Jesus instructing his followers to do, you will move closer to finding a deep sense of peace. For me, there were three teachings that were significant that I will highlight, as they're not necessarily obvious. If I hadn't noticed these three "patterns" of instruction I might have missed finding peace:

○ **Don't Worry:** More than once in the Gospels, Jesus teaches people not to worry, an invitation to let God provide, let God control. Activity 4.4 later in this chapter is designed to help you see the pattern of Jesus' invitation to not worry.

○ **Don't Be Afraid**: We humans are a fearful bunch. How many decisions do we each make every day out of fear, rather than love? How many of the words that come out of our mouths are based on fear, not love? Fear of what will happen, fear of what other people will think, fear of failure...fear, fear, fear. There are many occurrences of Jesus instructing people to not be afraid in the Gospels. It's the advice He gives most often in the Gospels. Unfortunately, looking at each of our actions and statements through the prism of fear provides understanding for most of our actions and statements. Activity 4.3 later in this chapter is designed to help you see the pattern of Jesus and God's invitation to not be afraid (other than the healthy fear of displeasing God).

○ **Serve Others**: A major cause of many of my problems earlier in life was an excessive focus on myself: my needs, my desires, and later, an excessive focus on my problems. Just shifting my focus from self to others had a huge impact on my peacefulness. William Law describes the connection between "self" and "sin": "self is the root and substance of all sin".[47] Just by changing our focus away from the self we accomplish a lot in the way of turning away from sin.

The simple but unexpected act of washing the feet of the apostles before the Last Supper is a powerful lesson in many ways for how we should live: serving others, doing what needs to be done and what others would rather not do, serving humbly, serving unexpectedly (in ways *other people* don't expect), but focusing on serving others rather than serving ourselves. There are many ways we can each serve one another at home, at work (or school), at church,

---

47 from *The Power of the Spirit* by William Law, page 35, copyright 1971 but originally written in the early 1700s. Thank you for the book Matthew.

and in the community. Some opportunities to serve others in ways they don't expect can be planned, others will just present themselves and if we have the right attitude we'll take advantage of the opportunity and perform the act of service. Activity 4.5 is designed to help you identify ways that you can serve others deliberately and unexpectedly, but be open to the opportunities that will surely arise that can't be planned.

If you go to school and try to enroll in an advanced Math or Science course but haven't taken the more fundamental courses that the advanced course is based upon, you'll be told that you need to take the "prerequisite" ("required before") courses first. The idea behind requiring students to take certain courses before they take other courses is based on the understanding that they won't understand the more advanced course if they haven't mastered the concepts and skills in the more foundational courses.

The same is true here with peace. I don't think it's possible for you to have a deep sense of peace without taking on BIG IDEAS 1 and 2 first, and then following Jesus' instructions for living found in the Gospels, especially those related to worry, fear and serving others. Depending on your personal circumstances, BIG IDEA #5 may also be a prerequisite to finding a deep sense of peace, but more on that in the next chapter.

* * *

Maintaining Peace in a Broken World

Once you realize a deep sense of peace, that peace will come under attack. It will come under attack by people: possibly by those close to you, possibly by complete strangers. You'll find yourself in circumstances where your deep sense of peace is challenged. You'll need to learn to not allow people or situations take you away from your deep sense of peace.

- When someone close to you is grumpy and says something unflattering or negative, when they do something that you perceive as inconsiderate, resist the temptation to respond in kind:
  - let it go, don't retaliate
  - see the person through God's eyes, pray for them
  - practice "immediate forgiveness" as descried in BIG IDEA #2
  - say something nice to them, or do something nice for them

- when someone you don't know does something unkind, resist the temptation to be offended:
  - see the experience as a clear marker of someone who could benefit from your guidance
  - practice "immediate forgiveness" as descried in BIG IDEA #2
  - say something nice to them, or do something nice for them

If you do find yourself taken away from your sense of peace, deliberately get back there: be thankful for the gift of God's Grace for all the hurts you have caused, deliberately forgive anyone who has taken you away from your sense of peace, spend some time reading the Gospels or watching a word-for-word Gospel DVD. Remember this guidance from the Apostle Paul in his letter to the Roman church:

> "Do not repay anyone evil for evil. Be careful to do what is right in the eyes of everybody. If it is possible, as far as it depends on you, live at peace with everyone. Do not take revenge, my friends, but leave room for God's wrath, for it is written: 'It is mine to avenge; I will repay,' says the Lord.

> "On the contrary: If your enemy is hungry, feed him; if he is thirsty, give him something to drink. In doing this, you will heap burning coals on his head. Do not be overcome by evil, but overcome evil with good."
> (Romans 12: 17-21, emphasis added)

When you find yourself moved away from your place of peace, quickly get back to that place. Try to get back quicker over time, so you spend less time removed from peace. Then work to not be taken from your place of peace in the first place. Develop your ability to immediately forgive with smaller hurts so that you are prepared to forgive immediately when faced with deeper hurts.

* * *

How I Missed BIG IDEA #4 as a Cradle Catholic
(and you may have too)

Here are the reasons that I missed BIG IDEA #4 as a Cradle Catholic:

Reason #1: I saw peace as an absence from war, not something within me.

Reason #2: I was surrounded by references to peace and never stopped to consider them.
In spite of the fact that I didn't understand the true meaning of peace, from the standpoint of Jesus, peace shows up in a variety of places in the Catholic Church. As a Cradle Catholic, here are some ways that we may have experienced peace in the Church:

"The Sign of Peace" Ritual at Every Mass
The most common and obvious place to find peace in the Catholic Church is in the Mass. Hundreds of millions of Catholics wish those around them "peace be with you" or, simply "peace" every weekend at mass around the world. How many of those Mass participants understand the significance of those words beyond well wishes for others? How many are at a deep state of peace?

I have wished more than 5,000 people "peace" at Mass over more than four decades[48]. Only a few hundred (the most recent ones) of those more than 5,000 people were people I wished to have peace and I actually understood what I was wishing them.

Lamb of God
At the start of every Mass, three simple lines are recited or sung, in Latin or English or the local language:

> Lamb of God, you take away the sins of the world, have mercy on us.
> Lamb of God, you take away the sins of the world, have mercy on us.
> Lamb of God, you take away the sins of the world, grant us peace.

If you're a Cradle Catholic, you've recited or sung these words at every Mass. The first two lines relate directly to BIG IDEA #1, as they describe Jesus, the sacrificial Lamb of God, in his role of taking away the world's sins, so that we can receive God's Grace, His forgiveness of our sins. The last line hints at the outcome of receiving God's Grace, receiving from God a sense of peace we couldn't realize in any other way. I believe that forgiveness of others, with no exceptions (BIG IDEA #2) is also a precondition to realizing Jesus' peace, even though it's not contained within the three lines of the Agnus Dei, it is clearly

---

48 I have gone to Mass at least 50 times each year I was actively part of a Catholic parish, I was active in the Catholic church
    for at least 25 years, and wished at least 5 people at each Mass "peace", "peace be with you", or something similar. 50 x 25 x
    5 = 6,250. This estimate is conservative and the actual number is probably higher.

spelled out by Jesus in Matthew 6:14-15.

Peace Banners in Sanctuaries

Many Christian churches of all denominations decorate their sanctuaries during Christmas and Easter with banners that include the word "Peace", or possibly "Paz" (Spanish) or perhaps Paix (French), or "Pax" (Latin) or any one of hundreds of other languages. My understanding of the word on the banners for most of my life was a desire for ending of wars, not something deeper and more personal. Not something specifically and directly tied to following Jesus, a state of being within myself.

Pax Christi Parishes

Many Catholic parishes have "peace" in their names: "Pax Christi" is a common enough parish name that most regions have at least one parish with that name. How many of the parishoners understand the underlying meaning of their parish name? The name is Latin for "Peace of Christ".

Reason #3: I missed BIG IDEA #'s 1-3

I missed finding a deep sense of peace because I hadn't taken on the first three BIG IDEAS. Once I did and started putting Jesus' teachings into practice, I found my way to a deep sense of peace and had an "Aha!" moment. Only then did I understand and appreciate all the references to peace growing up as a Cradle Catholic.

* * *

Taking on BIG IDEA #4: Find a Peace You've Never Known
A Simple Plan That Works

Here's a simple plan that provides the details for you to Find a Peace You've Never Known. It's based on what's worked for me.

As you work through the list, check off tasks as you complete them. The tasks are in an order that seems to make sense, but do them in any order that works for you. Add additional tasks if needed.

Task	Description	Investment	Complete?
☑ **Complete**	**Complete The Simple Plan for BIG IDEA # 1: Understand and Accept Grace** Knowing that God has forgiven you through Jesus' suffering and death for your sins is the first step in getting you to a deep sense of peace.	varies	☐
☑ **Complete**	**The Simple Plan for BIG IDEA # 2: Forgive Others – *No Exceptions*** Forgiving the hurts that others have inflicted on you in the past is a major step in getting to peace.	varies	☐
☑ **Complete**	**The Simple Plan for BIG IDEA # 3: Read & Study the Bible, *But Immerse Yourself in the Gospels*** Immersing yourself in the Gospels will have an effect on the way you think. There are a number of Jesus' teachings that if followed will lead you to the peace you have wished for others at Sunday Mass.	varies	☐
✍ **Activity**	**Complete Activity 4.1: Rate Your Current Level of Peace**	a few minutes	☐
✍ **Activity**	**Complete Activity 4.2: Identify People at Peace**	a few minutes	☐
✍ **Read**	**Read The key passages in the Bible that Describe Peace** [see the key passages in the Bible that describe peace later in this chapter]	2 – 4 hours	☐

Task	Description	Investment	Complete?
✍ Activity	**Complete Activity 4.3: Freedom from Fear Study & Pledge**	1 – 4 hours	☐
✍ Activity	**Complete Activity 4.4: Freedom from Worry Study & Pledge**	1 – 4 hours	☐
✍ Activity	**Complete Activity 4.4: Feet Washing Plan** Jesus instructed us to serve others. This will help you shift from focusing on yourself to focusing on others, a critical change to find peace. This is an activity that if done right you will never finish.	ongoing	☐
✍ Activity	**Complete Activity 4.6: Sermon on the Mount Top 3 List**	ongoing	☐
? Consider (Optional)	**If you've completed all of the tasks above and don't find a deep sense of peace, take a look at BIG IDEA #5: Consider Baptism in the next chapter.**	varies	☐
			☐
			☐
			☐
PLAN TOTAL		varies $0.00	☐

Activity 4.1: Rate Your Current Level of Peace

How to Complete this Activity: Consider your general emotional state. Read through the choices below and select the one that best fits your general emotional state, not necessarily how you feel right as this moment, but how you feel generally.

My Current Level of Peace

☐   I feel deeply distressed, troubled, tense or harried. I'm not well. I wouldn't wish my general emotional state on anyone.

☐   I'm not in crisis, but I don't feel at ease or at peace.

☐   I have glimpses of peace, but usually I'm tense or stressed.

☐   I feel a sense of peace.

☐   I feel an incredible sense of peace, a deep sense of peace. I want others to share the same.

* * *

☐   Other: _____

The ultimate goal is to experience a deep sense of peace. That's what you wished others in every Mass you ever attended.

* * *

Activity 4.2: Identify People at Peace

How to Complete this Activity: Have you known anyone in the Church that seemed to be at peace with God, with everyone else, with themselves, who lived life fully?

One of the priests in our parish growing up in the 1970s, Rev. Leonard Spanburgh[49], was one of those people. Looking back, he was probably a person that some would consider a "hippie". He clearly had a sense of peace about him. He was not unfamiliar with the drug scene, and helped heroin addicts overcome their addictions. Spanburgh was an artist: he painted and played electric guitar. He talked of going to Canada for an operation because they didn't allow the operation in the US without anesthetic drugs. He lived life "abundantly" and was "salt" and "light" to others. Spanburgh, with the benefit of hindsight, was probably experiencing a deep sense of peace.

Use the template below to identify people you have encountered in life that are truly at peace:

People at Peace
Have you ever encountered anyone that seemed to have a deep sense of peace? If so, list them here: _____ _____ _____   _____ _____ _____   Do you think they understood and accepted God's Grace? (BIG IDEA #1)   yes: ☐ no: ☐   Do you think they forgave others, without exception? (BIG IDEA #2)   yes: ☐ no: ☐   Do you think they were familiar with the Gospels at some degree of depth, do you think they "immersed" themselves in the Gospels? (BIG IDEA #3)   yes: ☐ no: ☐   What conclusions can you make based on this reflection?

---

49 We called him "Father Spanburgh" growing up, and most priests are referred to as "Father". Jesus taught in the Gospels, however, that there is only one "Father", God, and that we should call no man "Father". Note how some priests refer to themselves as "Reverend" rather than "Father". This is in keeping with Jesus' instruction.

RESOURCE: The Bible (key passages describing Jesus' peace)

Jesus, the "Prince of Peace"

Isaiah was written about 700 years before the birth of Jesus (c. 700-680 B.C.), and foretells of Jesus' birth, describing Jesus as the "Prince of Peace":

> ෨෪
> ### Jesus is the "Prince of Peace"
> ෨෪

"For unto us a child is born,
to us a son is given,
and the government will be on his shoulders.

And he will be called
Wonderful, Counselor, Mighty God,
Everlasting Father, Prince of Peace.

Of the increase of his government and peace
there will be no end." (Isaiah 9: 6-7)

From the beginning, Jesus' mission on Earth was directly tied to "peace." Isaiah refers to the coming savior of the world as the "Prince of Peace" and describes the outcome of his mission as increasing peace without end.

If you consider that everyone born could potentially experience Jesus' peace, there is no end to the increase in Jesus' peace, it's infinite, as long as new people are born into the world.

Jesus Speaks of Peace to his Disciples

Jesus wished his followers peace. In the Gospel of John, while Jesus is teaching and encouraging his disciples before he is arrested, right before being beaten and nailed to a cross, he tells them[50],

> *"Peace I leave with you, my peace I give you.*
> *I do not give as the world gives.*
> *Do not let your hearts be troubled and do not be afraid."*
> *(John 14: 27)*

Since these words are spoken right before Jesus is arrested, they must be important, along with other statements Jesus made before he was arrested, which he knew was about to happen.

"I do not give as the world gives" is a curious choice of words. My understanding is that Jesus was

---

50 John 14:27.

referring to His peace as eternal, whereas peace in this world between people and nations is typically fleeting.

"Blessed are the Peacemakers..."
At the beginning of the Sermon on the Mount, Matthew 5-7, Jesus taught the Beatitudes, eight statements that seem like paradoxes, and are difficult to understand. Onc of the Beatitudes, the seventh of eight, relates to peace:

> *"Blessed are the peacemakers,*
> *for they will be called sons of God."*

Many people, myself included, read this verse, Matthew 5: 9, and think of world peace, peace among nations. While that may be one level of meaning that Jesus intended, there's another level of meaning that's not so obvious. On the individual level, finding peace within yourself can only be found, I believe, if you take on BIG IDEA #'s 1, 2 and 3:

- understanding and then accepting God's forgiveness of your sins (BIG IDEA #1)
- forgiving others without exception (BIG IDEA #2)
- reading and studying the Bible and immersing yourself in the Gospels (BIG IDEA #3)

In immersing yourself in the Gospels I think you need to understand Jesus' invitation to live life without fear and without worry, with a focus on serving others. These specific teachings, once forgiveness is in place, help you find a deep sense of peace.

I don't think you can find the peace Jesus described if you don't do those things. But if you do these basic but important things, then I think peace is the natural outcome.

If you do find that deep sense of peace and if you help others find it too, you are a "peacemaker", and therefore you are a son or daughter of God. That's what I understand "Blessed are the peacemakers..." to mean.

* * *

Peace, "The fruit of the Spirit..."

In Paul's Letter to the Galatians, Paul contrasts the acts of our sinful nature with the fruit of the spirit. Paul describes the acts of our sinful nature[51]:

> *"The acts of the sinful nature are obvious: sexual immorality, impurity and debauchery, idolatry and witchcraft, hatred, discord, jealousy, fits of rage, selfish ambition, dissensions, factions and envy, drunkenness, orgies, and the like."*

Paul then goes on to describe what one can hope for after accepting Grace, being Baptized, and filled with the Spirit[52]:

> *"But the fruit of the Spirit is love, joy, **peace**, patience, kindness, goodness, faithfulness, gentleness, and self-control."*

So, if we "live by the Spirit" as Paul encourages, one of the outcomes of living by the spirit is "peace." BIG IDEA #'s 1, 2 and 3 (and for some people, BIG IDEA #5) are prerequisites for following Paul's encouragement to "live by the Spirit," but if realized, should lead to peace, as well as the other results or fruits of the Spirit.

* * *

---

51 Galatians 5: 19-21 (NIV).
52 Galatians 5: 22-23 (NIV).

Activity 4.3: Freedom from Fear Study & Pledge

How to Complete this Activity: God designed us and built us. As our designer and creator God knows that we have a tendency to be afraid, to harbor fear within us.

One major theme of the Bible is the invitation to not be afraid, to cast fear aside. Just realizing that we have a tendency toward fear, that it's not necessary, and that God invites us to not be afraid, can help us avoid fear.

Read and consider all of the occurrences of Jesus and Paul and Peter and John and God and Angels of God instructing people to not be afraid. These are just the occurrences in the New Testament. The Hebrew Bible includes the same pattern. We're invited to fear nothing (other than God, who we should love and respect, and have a healthy fear of displeasing):

Chapter/Verse	Chapter / Verse	Chapter / Verse
Matthew 10: 26-28	Luke 12: 4	Acts 27: 24 (Angel of God speaking)
Matthew 10:31	Luke 12: 7	Philippians 1: 28
Matthew 14: 27	Luke 12: 32	Hebrews 13: 6
Matthew 17: 7	Luke 21: 9	1 Peter 3: 6
Matthew 25: 25 (parable)	John 6: 20	1 Peter 3: 14
Matthew 28: 10	John 12: 15	1 John 4: 18
Mark 5: 36	John 14: 27	Revelation 1: 17
Mark 6: 50	Acts 18: 9 (God speaking in a dream)	Revelation 2: 10
Luke 8: 50	Acts 23: 11	* * *

Fear is a huge pattern in the Bible, but it's also a huge pattern in most people's lives. Use the template on the next page to record all of the occurrences of you or those around you making decisions or saying things out of fear rather than out of love:

Fear Log

Record your words and actions that are driven by fear here:

Date	Self or Others?	Words or Actions?	Description
_____	_____	_____	_____
_____	_____	_____	_____
_____	_____	_____	_____
_____	_____	_____	_____
_____	_____	_____	_____

Once you see the pattern of "don't be afraid" in the Bible and recognize the fear in your words, choices and actions and in the words, choices and actions of those around you, the next obvious question is: "how do I not be afraid?" God has been described as "love." Love and fear are opposed to one another. Decide to choose to act and speak in love rather than fear. Decide to put your trust in God, not yourself, which is limited.

My experience is that it's easier to be free from fear if you've taken on the first three BIG IDEAS, but it also involves a deliberate choice to not be afraid and requires you to trust in God.

Use the pledge below to help you make the deliberate choice to not live in fear. Not living in fear is a requirement to finding the peace that Jesus and Paul and Peter describe and that you have wished hundreds of others as a Cradle Catholic at Sunday Mass:

Love Not Fear Pledge

Yes, I, _____, choose to not live a life in fear. I accept God's invitation to "not be afraid." I will trust God and let go of all fears, except one: my "fear" of God: a deep respect and love for God; that is, a fear of displeasing Him.

I realize that most people in the world say things based on fear not based on love. I realize that most people in the world make decisions or take action based on fear not based on love. I will strive to speak, make decisions, and take actions based on love, not based on fear.

Signed: _____   Date: _____

Activity 4.4: Freedom from Worry Study & Pledge

How to Complete this Activity: God designed us and built us. As our designer and creator God knows that we have a tendency to be worriers.

One major theme of the Bible is the invitation to not worry. Just realizing that we have a tendency toward worry, that worry isn't necessary, and that God invites us to not worry, can help us avoid worry.

Read and consider all of the occurrences of Jesus and Paul and Peter instructing us, inviting us to be free from worry:

Chapter/Verse	Chapter / Verse	Chapter / Verse
Matthew 6:25-34	Mark 13: 11	Philippians 4: 6
Matthew 10: 19	Luke 12: 22-26	1 Peter 3: 14
Matthew 15: 14	Luke 21: 14	* * *

Use the template below to record everything you're worried about right now or that you have a tendency to worry about:

Worry Log
Record your worries here:
_____
_____
_____
_____
_____

So "how do I stop worrying?" Decide to put your trust in God, not yourself, which is limited. "Let go, let God" as some people say.

My experience is that it's easier to be free from worry if you've taken on the first three BIG IDEAS, but it also involves a deliberate choice to trust in God.

Use the pledge below to help you make the deliberate choice to not worry. Not worrying is a requirement to finding the peace that Jesus and Paul and Peter describe and that you have wished hundreds of others as a Cradle Catholic at Sunday Mass:

Pledge to Not Worry

Yes, I, _____, choose to not worry. I accept God's invitation to be free from worry. I will trust God and rely upon Him to provide.

Signed: _____   Date: _____

---

* * *

Activity 4.5: Feet Washing Plan

How to Complete this Activity: Jesus washed the feet of the Apostles to show how we should live: serving others, doing what many would prefer not to do but has value, doing something that if we didn't do it wouldn't get done, being humble, and doing the unexpected. Shifting your focus from yourself to others and focusing on serving is a critical ingredient to finding a deep sense of peace. Use the template below to plan how you can serve others at home, at work (or school), at church, and in the community. You may already have "assigned" service obligations, find ways of doing those well but also doing the unexpected. Be open to opportunities to serve that cannot be planned. Humbly avoid calling attention to your deliberate and unexpected acts of service, but you don't need to be secretive. You may inspire others to do the same.

Area	Deliberate & Unexpected Acts of Service	Complete?
Home	1. 2. 3.	☐ ☐ ☐
Work/School	1. 2. 3.	☐ ☐ ☐
Church	1. 2. 3.	☐ ☐ ☐
Community	1. 2. 3.	☐ ☐ ☐

Activity 4.6: Sermon on the Mount Top 3 List

How to Complete this Activity: Go back to *Activity 3.2: Jesus' Instructions for Living* and review the instructions you identified as needing improvement. Pick the three you need to work on most, the ones with the biggest room for improvement. List them below. Identify one to three specific actions you'll take that will help you put each instruction into practice. Then go do it, complete the plan. Once you've mastered these three, choose three more. Continue the process until you've aligned your life with all of Jesus' teachings in the Sermon on the Mount. Also look to Jesus' teachings elsewhere in the Gospels.

Chapter/Verse	Jesus' Instruction for Living	Complete?
	Instruction: _____ Supporting Actions: 1. _____ 2. _____ 3. _____	☐
	Instruction: _____ Supporting Actions: 1. _____ 2. _____ 3. _____	☐
	Instruction: _____ Supporting Actions: 1. _____ 2. _____ 3. _____	☐

BIG IDEA #5:
Consider Baptism

Then Jesus came from Galilee to the
Jordan to be Baptized by John. But John tried to
deter him, saying, "I need to be baptized by you,
and do you come to me?"

Jesus replied, "Let it be so now; it is
proper for us to do this to fulfill all
righteousness." Then John consented.

As soon as Jesus was baptized, he went up out
of the water. At that moment heaven was
opened, and he saw the Spirit of God
descending like a dove and lighting on him. And
a voice from heaven said, "This is my Son,
whom I love; with him am I well pleased."

The Gospel of Matthew, Chapter 2, verses 13-17 (NIV)

BIG IDEA #5: Consider Baptism

> ಬಂಡ
>
> **Did Jesus need to be baptized?**
>
> **Certainly not. Yet He was anyway.**
>
> ಬಂಡ

Did Jesus need to be baptized? Certainly not. Yet He was anyway.

There it is in the Gospels, Jesus deliberately chose to be baptized: he was immersed in the Jordan River by John[53].

Three years ago I studied the occurrences of baptism in the Bible with our pastor over the course of a few weeks. We looked at all of the places where baptism is described in the Gospels and the Book of Acts. A few things made an impression on me:

Jesus as the Ultimate Role Model: Jesus didn't need to be baptized, but he chose to be baptized by John. It marked an important change in his life, it was the start of his ministry of about three years which led to his death and resurrection.

The Ethiopian Eunuch's Childlike Faith: The Ethiopian eunuch who Phillip helped understand the Good News saw water and said, "Look, there is water. What is to prevent my being baptized?" (Acts 8:34, NABRE) and Philip baptized the eunuch.

> ಬಂಡ
>
> **"Look, there is water.**
>
> **What is to prevent my being baptized?"**
>
> ಬಂಡ

The Great Commission's Linking of Baptism and Discipleship: Jesus gave specific instructions to the eleven apostles[54] right before he was taken up into heaven. The specific instructions are known as "The Great Commission." Jesus instructs the apostles: "All authority in heaven and on earth has been given to me. Therefore go and make disciples of all nations, baptizing them in the name of the Father and of the Son and of the Holy Spirit, and teaching them to obey everything I have commanded you. And surely I am with you always, to the very end of the age." (Matthew 28: 18-20, NIV)

While we read and discussed all the occurrences of baptism in the New Testament, these three Bible passages made an impression on me and convinced me of my need to be baptized.

---

53 See the Gospel of Matthew, Chapter 3, verses 13-17; also the Gospel of Mark, Chapter 1, verses 1-12; and the Gospel of Luke, Chapter 3, verses 21-23.

54 After Judas Iscariot died and before Barnabas was made an Apostle.

I have a document, a "Certificate of Baptism" that states that I was baptized on March 5, 1967, about four weeks after birth.

A copy of that document is reproduced on this page[55]. Catholics believe that baptism is so important that babies should be baptized soon after birth.

While I have the document "certifying" that I was baptized in 1967, for most of my life:

- I didn't understand the Good News; I didn't understand God's Grace through Jesus' death and resurrection, and my need for Grace

- I didn't realize I was required to forgive others, transmitting God's Grace to me onto all others

- I had only a passing understanding of the New Testament and didn't deliberately strive to live my life according to the teachings of Jesus.

- The Holy Spirit wasn't dwelling within me.

Certificate of Baptism

St. Catherine of Siena Church
339 POMPTON AVENUE
CEDAR GROVE, NEW JERSEY 07009

→ **This is to Certify** ←

That *Patrick James Mc Garrity*
Child of *Joseph R.*
and *Patricia Murphy*
born in *Montclair, New Jersey*
on the *4th* day of *February*, *1967*
was **Baptized**
on the *5th* day of *March*, *1967*
According to the Rite of the Roman Catholic Church
by the Rev. *Richard McGuinness*
the Sponsors being _____

as appears from the Baptismal Register of this Church.

Dated *March 31, 2003*

Charles W. G....
Pastor

NO. 314 F.J. REMEY CO. Inc. MINEOLA, NY

---

55 My "Sponsors" or godparents listed on the certificate have been obscured out of respect for them. Many godparents, including myself, could do better, so these two people are not acting in a way different from many godparents.

Jesus as the Ultimate Role Model

As I studied the occurrences of baptism in the Bible, I realized that in the same way Jesus didn't *need to* be baptized, I didn't *need to* be baptized. But...in the same way Jesus felt called to be baptized and felt an inner need to be baptized, I too felt called to be baptized and felt an inner need to be baptized.

Jesus' actions of 2,000 years ago were an invitation to me to follow my heart. To choose love, not give in to fear. What fears? Here are a few that I considered that you may encounter if you consider baptism:

Fear of what the Catholic Church might think. Not knowing specifics at the time, I suspected the Catholic Church would not approve if I chose to be baptized as an adult, having been baptized as a month old baby. I also suspected they might not be excited about the baptism taking place at a non-denominational Christian church. While I wasn't afraid of what the Catholic Church would think if I decided to be baptized, what the Church thought did occur to me, and the opportunity to be fearful was there. For some people this might be a significant concern. Don't let fear affect your decision, other than the fear (or reverence) for God, and the desire to follow Jesus' teachings and follow Jesus as a role model.

Fear of what my family might think. I never met one of the two "sponsors" or Godparents listed on my baptismal certificate. The other sponsor I knew but I've never had a faith-based conversation with them at any time. I wasn't concerned about what they might think of my adult Baptism. My Mother, on the other hand, had seen to it that we went to church every week – every week. I can't say that I missed church once while living in the home in New Jersey in which I grew up. She sacrificed so that we could all go to Catholic high schools. Mom leads a life in keeping with the teachings of Jesus. Mom is an example of someone who has found peace within the Catholic Church. She goes to church pretty much every day. Mom is involved in charitable causes some of which we only learn about when she receives an award and an article lists her accomplishments. If I harbored a fear of what anyone in my family would think, that would be my Mother. While I considered what my Mother would think, it didn't affect my decision. Don't let concern or fear of what a family member might think affect your decision either.

Fear of standing and speaking in front of a few hundred people. Having witnessed a number of baptisms of adults, I knew that I would be speaking in front of a group of a few hundred people. While surveys show[56] many people fear public speaking more than anything else, and while I did consider the need to speak in front of a large group of people, I didn't let that affect my decision. Don't let this affect your decision either.

Choosing Love not Fear

What love? How would I be choosing to be baptized as an adult out of love, and not out of fear? By taking a risk while also following Jesus' lead.

---

56 See the article accessed on May 28, 2015 from http://artofpublicspeaking.net/fear-of-public-speaking-statistics/ that describes "Glossophobia", the fear of public speaking as being the most commonly cited fear, ahead of the fears of Death, Spiders, Darkness, Heights, Social Situations, Flying, etc.

The Ethiopian Eunuch's Child-like Faith

The Ethiopian eunuch's question "Look, there is water. What is to prevent my being baptized?" made me ask the same question of myself. Why shouldn't I be baptized? The Ethiopian Eunuch was a man of action. He managed the affairs of the Queen of his country. He didn't ponder, he didn't debate, he didn't second guess himself. He heard the Good News, he understood its key points, he accepted the gift. He understood the role of Jesus as leader, and followed His lead. The Eunuch's faith was "child like" in it's simplicity, in it's openness, in its directness.

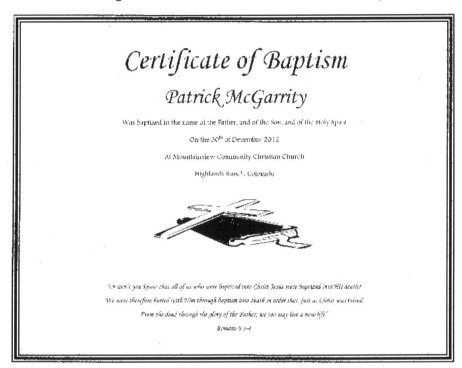

As I studied the occurrences of baptism in the Bible with Pastor Mark, I could think of a lot of reasons why I should be baptized. It's what Jesus did. I had supported others getting baptized, but hadn't done the same thing myself. I had developed a new understanding of the Gospel, including the importance of Grace and had accepted it really for the first time. I developed a deep appreciation for the importance of forgiving others in all cases, and the incredible power when forgiveness wins. I understood the deep, very deep wisdom of requiring all to forgive all. I had recently for the first time read all four Gospels at least once, reading each completely within a few days. I had watched word-for-word DVD performances of Mark, John, Matthew and Acts a few times, immersing myself in the Gospels and Acts to the point of being able to draw upon key passages in my mind as opportunities arose.

The only reason I could think of for not being baptized was that I had a certificate saying that I was baptized in 1967 at the age of four weeks, and had a suspicion that the Catholic Church wouldn't approve. Not enough negatives to outweigh the positives.

The Great Commission's Linking of Baptism and Discipleship

Baptism and discipleship are clearly linked in Jesus' final instructions in the Great Commission.

Doesn't it seem likely that Jesus would applaud anyone who, even though they were baptized as an infant, decided to be baptized as an adult, publicly confessing their faith, after recently understanding and accepting God's Grace, after recently understanding the absolute requirement to forgive others in all cases, after recently reading all of each of the Gospels for the first time? Wouldn't Jesus applaud such a choice? I know he would.

With Jesus and the Ethiopian eunuch as inspiration, I decided that I too needed to be baptized. I know the exact moment the decision was made.

Within a week I was baptized in the pool at our non-denominational church, December 30, 2012.

I took care to write out and memorize my declaration of accepting Jesus and his gift of Grace, to sharing his death on the cross and new life through resurrection, to living my life as a follower of Him. I made my declaration boldly.

December 30, 2012. That day I was baptized and that day means more to me than my birthday, February 4th, 1967. I don't do much to celebrate my birthday, trying to downplay it as much as possible. But I do actively celebrate my re-birthday, as in retrospect it was a turning point in my life. I do sense that not long after my re-birth I was filled with the Holy Spirit. I don't believe that was the case before December 2012.

I can now state without hesitation that following the lead of Jesus and the Ethiopian eunuch and undergoing baptism in 2012 was the right thing to do. Originally, there were only 4 BIG IDEAS. I developed a deck of PowerPoint charts and shared what I had learned about the first four BIG IDEAS with other Cradle Catholics, usually at Starbucks or Panera.

About six months after my baptism, the 4 BIG IDEAS became the 5 BIG IDEAS. I realized the importance of considering baptism as an adult being an important consideration for Cradle Catholics. It may not be right for all Cradle Catholics, that's why it's titled "Consider Baptism" rather than "Be Baptized." You need to decide for yourself what's right, but don't decide out of fear, decide out of love and understanding. This chapter is intended to help you with that decision, but listen to God for guidance.

Jesus' View on Baptism

Jesus' view on Baptism is that it's required. His view on Baptism is revealed in two Gospel passages: his own Baptism and his meeting with Nicodemus at night as described in the Gospel of John, both of which are reproduced below.

John was surprised that Jesus wanted to be Baptized by him, but honored Jesus' request. Jesus' Baptism represented a turning point in Jesus' life, it kicked off his ministry and within a few years he was tortured, crucified and rose from the dead.

Surprised to Realize I Had a Connection with Amish and Mennonite Christians

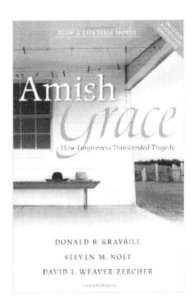

After choosing to be baptized as Jesus was baptized, as an adult, by choice, publicly confessing my faith, I read the book *Amish Grace, How Forgiveness Transcended Tragedy* by Donald Kraybill, Steven Nolt and David Weaver-Zercher (see additional description of the book in BIG IDEA #2).

The book describes the Nickel Mines school shooting. It focuses on the unusual[57] reaction of the Amish to forgive the shooter and his family. In describing the Amish and their living out their Christian beliefs, the authors describe the early history of the Amish and Mennonite communities in Europe. Growing up in New Jersey, I was familiar with the Amish in Lancaster County, in rural Pennsylvania. In our travels through Pennsylvania we stopped a few times at the family style restaurants found in Lancaster County run by the Amish.

I didn't realize, however, that many of the early Amish and Mennonites were persecuted by Catholics *and* Lutherans in Europe for deciding to be baptized as adults, even through they were baptized in the Catholic Church as infants.

I was surprised at my connection with the Amish and Mennonite Christians, surprised and humbled. The decision I made a few months earlier to be baptized as an adult, the decision I struggled with a bit and which I subsequently realized was absolutely the right thing to do, others paid for the same decision with their lives. Hundreds of Amish and Mennonite Christians were persecuted and murdered by Catholics and Lutherans which sought to protect the Catholic and Lutheran Churches from "heresy". Can you imagine any follower of Jesus advocating the murder of other Christians because they interpreted Scripture differently and acted on their

Illustration 1: Execution of Anneken Hendriks in 1571, as portrayed by artist Jan Luyken in the book Martyr's Mirror in the 1600s.

---

57 A subsequent school shooting in Colorado in which a young, female high school student was shot by a classmate saw the family forgive quickly. More recently the families of the victims of the Bible Study shooting in South Carolina also expressed forgiveness quickly: at the accused's bail hearing. They followed-up the forgiveness with acts of kindness.

beliefs? To anyone who has read Jesus' Sermon on the Mount, Matthew chapters 5 through 7, the action clearly goes against Jesus' very specific instructions for how we should live. Jesus calls us to pray for our enemies, not murder them. If Catholics and Lutherans of the 1500s and 1600s believed that the Amish and Mennonite followers of Jesus were enemies, they should've prayed for them, not burned them to death. True to Jesus' teachings, the Amish and Mennonite peoples forgave their persecutors. Who do you think was on the side of God in that disagreement?

A large book that details the martyrs of that 1524 to 1660 period, *Martyr's Mirror*[58], walks through the Christian martyrs from the time of Christ through this period of "Christians" murdering Christians. The reason for their martyrdom? They were living out their life in a way they believed was and is aligned with Jesus' teachings.

The engraving on the previous page depicts a woman, Anneken Hendriks, who was murdered for her Christian beliefs and practices in Amsterdam, Holland, in 1571. Anneken was charged with heresy, as she left the Catholic church six years previously and joined a group of Mennonite Christians. Anneken was tried, found guilty, and sentenced for the "crimes" of failing to go to Catholic Confession or Catholic Communion for six years, and for the "crime" of deciding to be baptized as an adult after making a public statement, or "confession" as Martyr's Mirror calls it, of faith which she didn't do, she was incapable of doing, when she was previously baptized as an infant. It's incredible that Anneken's sentence for all of these "crimes" was a death sentence. *Martyr's Mirror* reproduces Anneken's sentencing decree from the City of Amsterdam's criminal court archives:

> "Whereas, Anna Heyndricks daughter, alias, Anna de Vlaster, formerly citizeness of this city, at present a prisoner here, mindful of her soul's salvation, and the obedience which she owed to our mother, the holy church, and to his royal majesty, as her natural lord and prince, rejecting the ordinances of the holy church, has neither been to confession, nor to the holy worthy sacrament, for six or seven years...

> ...and has further, about three years ago, forsaking and renouncing the baptism in her infancy from the holy church, been rebaptized, and then received the breaking of bread according to the manner on the Mennonist sect...

> ...therefore, my lord of the court, having heard the demand of my lord the bailiff, seen the confession of the prisoner, and having had regard to her obstinacy and stubbornness, have condemned her, and condemn her by these presents, to be, according to the decrees of his royal majesty, executed with fire, and declare all her property confiscated for the benefit of

---

58 full title of Martyr's Mirror and authorship from the title page: [title:] *The Bloody Theater or Martyr's Mirror of the Defenseless Christians*. [subtitle:] *Who Baptized Only Upon Confession of Faith, and Who Suffered and Died for the Testimony of Jesus, Their Savior, From the Time of Christ to the Year A.D. 1660.* [authorship:] *Compiled from Various Authentic Chronicles, Memorials and Testimonies by Thieleman J. van Braght. Translated from the Original Dutch or Holland Language from the Edition of 1660 by Joseph F. Sohm. Illustrations by Jan Luyken.* [end title page quote] The book is commonly found in the homes of Amish and Mennonite Christians. The book is large, more than 1,100 pages. It's available on Amazon and elsewhere.

his majesty aforesaid. Done in court, on the 10th of November, in the year 1571, in the presence of the judges, by the advice of all the burgomasters, in my knowledge, as secretary, and as was subscribed: [signed]W. PIETERS"

(excerpts from the Court Order reproduced on page 874 of *Martyr's Mirror*)

In fulfilling the court's sentencing, Anneken's mouth was stuffed with gunpowder, her hands were tied to a ladder, and she was tipped into a raging fire and burned to death. Why did she receive such treatment? Because she lived her life in a way that she believed was aligned with the teachings of Jesus, not another person or group's understanding of how to live. With the benefit of time, it seems that Anneken had a better understanding of Jesus' teachings than her accusers. Anneken's story is just one of hundreds, possibly thousands, of such stories in *Martyr's Mirror*.

> ℘)(℘
>
> **...few if any people at Mass realize the significance of [that one line in the Profession of Faith: "one baptism for the forgiveness of sins"]... I hear the fear that led to the hate that led to the mass murders...**
>
> ℘)(℘

Why bring up atrocities from the past? If you've worked through the BIG IDEAS and are now considering baptism, realize that hundreds, possibly thousands of people felt so strongly of the need to be baptized as an adult as Jesus was baptized, even though they were baptized as an infant, that they paid for the decision with their lives. If you're considering baptism as an adult, spend some time reading the accounts of people who were burned to death because they chose to do what you're considering. If you care about what the Catholic church thinks (many readers of this book who have left the Church may not, some readers may), realize that Pope John Paul II gave a general apology to the Mennonites for the actions of the Catholic Church during this period. Also realize that Pope Benedict, when a Cardinal, indicated at a conference in Germany that perhaps the beliefs of the Mennonites were more aligned with the teachings of Jesus than the actions of Catholics and the Catholic Church in the period[59]. Realize that in 2010 the Lutheran Church formally apologized for its persecution of Mennonite Christians. The Amish and Mennonite Christians forgave their persecutors long ago, but their choices to be baptized as adults after confessing their faith is a strong testimony that may help. Listen and look for God's help in making your decision.

* * *

---

[59] See https://www.goshen.edu/mqr/pastissues/jan99kauff.html *The Mennonite Quarterly Review*, January 1999: "Mennonite-Catholic Conversations in North America: History, Convergences, Opportunities", by Ivan J. Kauffman.

A Heightened Appreciation for the United States of America

One of the things that makes America great is that the persecution and execution of people for their religious beliefs that was prevalent in Europe in the 1500s and 1600s and which is present today in parts of Syria and Iraq are prohibited in this country. The First Amendment to the United States Constitution guarantees your right to be baptized without danger to your personal safety:

> "Congress shall make no law respecting an establishment of religion, or prohibiting the free exercise thereof"

ဘာ

...the same decision I made to be baptized as an adult others had paid for the same decision with their lives...

ဘာ

It hit me that the same decision I made to be baptized as an adult others had paid for the same decision with their lives, many suffering a painful death of being burned alive. I thought about the founding of the United States. People flocked to America from Europe for a variety of reasons. Most of my ancestors came to America because they were starving in Ireland. Many come to America because of the economic opportunities found here. But one major reason to leave Europe and come to America in the 1600s and later was the opportunity to exercise one's religious beliefs without the threat of persecution[60]. That protection was written into the Constitution by amendment in 1791.

While the President of the United States is powerful, as is the Congress, and as are the Justices of the Supreme Court, they all work for the Constitution. As powerful as each is, they must all honor the Constitution, including the religious freedoms guaranteed by it. Whether you choose to be baptized or not, if you are even considering being baptized, thank God that you live in a country that honors your right to make that choice, should you feel called to do so. Others did not enjoy the same freedom, and many suffered torture and murder by burning as a result.

* * *

---

60 Visitors to Colonial Williamsburg are reminded of how early America didn't get it all right: for example, in the Colony of Virginia, Catholics could not be a witness in a court case, could not vote, and could not hold office.

Taking on BIG IDEA #5: Consider Baptism
A Simple Plan that Works

Here's a simple plan that provides the details for you to Consider Baptism. It's based on the things that I did to better understand baptism and determine whether it was the right thing for me to do. The tasks are in an order that seems to make sense, but do them in any order that makes sense to you. Add additional tasks as appropriate.

Task	Description	Investment	Complete?
Read	**Read & Study the Bible Verses Describing Jesus' Baptism by John[61]** [see the Bible verses later in this chapter]	30-60 minutes	☐
Read	**Read & Study the Bible Verses Describing What Jesus Said About Baptism** [see the Bible verses later in this chapter]	30-60 minutes	☐
▶ DVD ▶ **Watch**	**Watch Jesus teaching Nicodemus on the Gospel of John DVD** (John 3: 1-22, view multiple times)	30-60 minutes	☐ ☐ ☐
Read	**Read & Study the Bible Verses Describing People Who Were Baptized** [see the Bible verses later in this chapter]	30-60 minutes	☐
Obtain	**Obtain Your Baptismal Certificate** If you were baptized in the Catholic Church, there is a record of your Baptism. Start with the church your family attended when you were young.	2 hours	☐

---

61 these verses are from the NIV translation.

Task	Description	Investment	Complete?
? **Evaluate**	**Evaluate Your Baptismal Certificate** After you have obtained your Baptismal Certificate, consider the following questions: • Do you know your Godparents? • Did your Godparents ever even have a conversation with you regarding Jesus? God? Have they ever guided you in your spiritual development? • Do you feel like the Holy Spirit has been guiding or helping you in your life?	30 minutes	☐
? **Evaluate**	**Your Place in Your Faith Journey (part 1)** If you have taken on the first three BIG IDEAS and sense that your life is changing, consider the following questions: • Do you understand the "Good News" in a way you never have before? • Do you accept God's gift of Grace? • Do you understand the need for you to forgive all others and are you willing to do that, with help? • Have you read and studied the Gospels for the first time?	varies	☐
? **Evaluate**	**Your Place in Your Faith Journey (part 2)** If you have taken on the first four BIG IDEAS, consider the following questions: • Do you feel more of a sense of peace than before, but feel that you could find deeper levels of peace? • Do you not feel any sense of peace?	varies	☐

Task	Description	Investment	Complete?
👂 👁 **Pray, Listen & Watch**	**Pray for guidance from God as to whether you should be baptized.** Listen and watch for God's response.	varies	☐
Talk	**Talk with a Priest or Deacon or Pastor in and/or out of the Catholic Church about Baptism** Share your faith journey with the person. Describe where you are now and your thoughts related to baptism as an adult, after confessing your faith. See where the conversation goes.	varies	☐
Be Thankful	**If you live in the United States and are considering baptism, be thankful** If you live in the United States or another country which protects religious freedom, thank God that you live in a country that allows you to even consider such a choice as being baptized without concern of potential harm coming to you (beheading in current times, burning at the stake in the 1600s, etc.). Many people fled Europe to escape torture and death for considering and acting on the choice to be baptized as an adult by choice, fully immersed in water, just as Jesus was baptized.	varies	☐
			☐
			☐
			☐
PLAN TOTAL		a few hours $0.00	☐

Baptism in the Gospels

The Baptism of Jesus

If you're looking to learn about baptism, the verses in the Bible that relate to the baptism of Jesus are certainly important:

Matthew 3:13-17

Then Jesus came from Galilee to the Jordan to be baptized by John. But John tried to deter him, saying, "I need to be baptized by you, and do you come to me?"

Jesus replied, "Let is be so now; it is proper for us to do this to fulfill all righteousness." Then John consented.

As soon as Jesus was baptized, he went up out of the water. At that moment heaven was opened, and he saw the Spirit of God descending like a dove and lighting on him. And a voice from heaven said, "This is my Son, whom I love; with him I am well pleased."

Mark 1:9-12

At that time Jesus came from Nazareth in Galilee and was baptized by John in the Jordan. As Jesus was coming up out of the water he saw heaven being torn open and the Spirit descending on him like a dove. And a voice came from heaven: "You are my Son, whom I love; with you I am well pleased."

At once the Spirit sent him out into the desert, and he was in the desert forty days, being tempted by Satan. He was with wild animals, and angels attended him.

After John was put in prison, Jesus went to Galilee, proclaiming the good news of God. "The time has come," he said. "The kingdom of God is near. Repent and believe in the good news!"

Luke 3:21-23

When all of the people were being baptized, Jesus was baptized too. And as he was praying, heaven was opened and the Holy Spirit descended on him in bodily form like a dove. And a voice came from heaven: "You are my Son, whom I love; with you I am well pleased."

Now Jesus himself was about thirty years old when he began his ministry.

Jesus' Teaching on Baptism

Jesus' teachings on baptism are also important if you're looking to understand baptism. Nicodemus, a Jewish leader in Jerusalem, came to Jesus secretly one night to ask him questions and be taught by Jesus:

Jesus Teaches Nicodemus Secretly
John 3: 1-6

Now there was a man of the Pharisees named Nicodemus, a member of the Jewish ruling council. He came to Jesus at night and said, "Rabbi, we know you are a teacher who has come from God. For no one could perform the miraculous signs you are doing if God were not with him."

In reply Jesus declared, "I tell you the truth, no one can see the kingdom of God unless he is born again."

"How can a man be born when he is old?" Nicodemus asked. "Surely he cannot enter a second time into his mother's womb to be born!"

Jesus answered, "I tell you the truth, no one can enter the kingdom of God unless he is born of water and the Spirit. Flesh gives birth to flesh, but the Spirit gives birth to spirit."

Jesus instructed his disciples to go out into the world and evangelize. Jesus linked baptism to discipleship, teaching people to obey Jesus' commands:

"The Great Commission"
Matthew 28:18-20

Then Jesus came to them and said, "All authority in heaven and on earth has been given to me. Therefore go and make disciples of all nations, baptizing them in the name of the Father and of the Son and of the Holy Spirit, and teaching them to obey everything I have commanded you. And surely I am with you always, to the very end of the age."

* * *

Bible Verses Describing People Who Were Baptized

In addition to the account of Jesus' baptism, there are descriptions in Acts of the Apostles of people being baptized:

"Peter Shares the Good News and about 3,000 are baptized"
Acts 2:36-41

"Therefore let all Israel be assured of this: God has made this Jesus, whom you crucified, both Lord and Christ."

When the people heard this, they were cut to the heart and said to Peter and the other apostles, "Brothers, what shall we do?"

Peter replied, "Repent and be baptized every one of you, in the name of Jesus Christ for the forgiveness of your sins. And you will receive the gift of the Holy Spirit. The promise is for you and your children and for all who are far off – for all whom the Lord our God will call."

With many other words he warned them; and he pleaded with them, "Save yourselves from this corrupt generation." Those who accepted his message were baptized, and about three thousand were added to their number that day.

* * *

"Philip Baptizes the Ethiopian Eunuch"
Acts 8:26-39

Now an angel of the Lord said to Philip, "Go south to the road – the desert road – that goes down from Jerusalem to Gaza." So he started out, and on his way he met an Ethiopian eunuch, an important official in charge of all the treasury of Candace, queen of the Ethiopians. This man had gone to Jerusalem to worship and on his way home was sitting in his chariot reading the book of Isaiah the prophet. The Spirit told Philip, "Go to that chariot and stay near it."

Then Philip ran up to the chariot and heard the man reading Isaiah the prophet. "Do you understand what you are reading?" Philip asked.

"How can I," he said, "unless someone explains it to me?" So he invited Philip to come up and sit with him.

The eunuch was reading this passage of Scripture:

"He was led like a sheep to the slaughter,
and as a lamb before the shearer is silent,
so he did not open his mouth.
In his humiliation he was deprived of justice.
  Who can speak of his descendants?
  For his life was taken from the earth.

The eunuch asked Philip, "Tell me please, who is the prophet talking about, himself or someone else?"   Then Philip began with that very passage of Scripture and told him the good news about Jesus.

As they traveled along the road they came to some water and the eunuch said, "Look, here is water. Why shouldn't I be baptized?" And he gave orders to stop the chariot. Then both Philip and the eunuch went down into the water and Philip baptized him. When they came up out of the water, the Spirit of the Lord suddenly took Philip away, and the eunuch did not see him again, but went on his way rejoicing.

* * *

NEXT:
Next Steps

"My dear brothers, take note of this: Everyone should be quick to listen, slow to speak and slow to become angry, for a man's anger does not bring about the righteous life that God desires.

Therefore, get rid of all moral filth and the evil that is so prevalent and humbly accept the word planted in you, which can save you.

Do not merely listen to the word, and so deceive yourselves. Do what it says.

Anyone who listens to the word but does not do what it says is like a man who looks at his face in the mirror and, after looking at himself, goes away and immediately forgets what he looks like.

But the man who looks intently into the perfect law that gives freedom, and continues to do this, not forgetting what he has heard, but doing it – he will be blessed in what he does."

James, Chapter 1, verses 19-25 (emphasis added)

NEXT: Next Steps

"Do what it says." So few words, such a challenge to accomplish, such a magnificent result and impact if done.

Once you've taken the time to understand the 5 BIG IDEAS, the next step is to put them into practice, or as James describes: "Do what it says":

- **BIG IDEA #1: Understand and Accept Grace:** For most people, this is straightforward to do, and you may have accepted God's Grace already. If you haven't, work at this until you can accept God's gift to you: Jesus paid for your sins 2,000 years ago. You are forgiven by God.

- **BIG IDEA #2: Forgive Others – *No Exceptions*:** Forgiveness of others is a requirement, not an option. Identify all of the unforgiveness in your heart that has built up so far in your life. Work to forgive all others. Going forward, work to build the habit of forgiving immediately. Strive to follow-up all decisions to forgive with intentional acts of kindness or love to "perfect", "seal" or "lock in" your forgiveness.

- **BIG IDEA #3: Read & Study the Bible, *But Immerse Yourself in the Gospels*:** By immersing yourself in the Gospels using the recommendations in this book, you'll be able to access relevant Gospel passages as you live your life. Accessing the Gospels as you go about your day will be a part of your transformation.

  Once you find a deep sense of peace you can expand out from the Gospels to the other parts of the New Testament as well as the Hebrew Bible.

- **BIG IDEA #4: Find a Peace You've Never Known:** BIG IDEAS 1, 2 and 3 will drive you to a place of peace with a few additional tasks in BIG IDEA #4. If you have worked to "do" or put into place the tasks in BIG IDEAS numbers 1 through 4 and don't feel at peace, seriously consider Baptism, BIG IDEA #5.

- **BIG IDEA #5: Consider Baptism:** To "do" this BIG IDEA, consider meeting with a priest if you are still in the Catholic Church or a pastor of another Christian denomination. If the Catholic priest will not discuss this with you or seriously consider your Baptism as an option because you were already Baptized as an infant, find another Priest. If that gets you nowhere, find a Pastor of another church that's not Catholic.

You can spend a lifetime working to "Do what it says" in the teachings of Jesus found in the Bible. This book is focused on the basics of getting you going in the right direction. It takes notice of your Catholic upbringing, and makes use of it in your transformation.

The 5 BIG IDEAS are not the end but mark the end of a very important beginning.

* * *

Here are some other things you can "do" that are "Next Steps" for anyone who has successfully put the 5 BIG IDEAS into practice:

- Lead a family member or friend in the study of the 5 BIG IDEAS and help them transform their lives.

- Conduct a 5 BIG IDEAS workshop for the Cradle Catholics in your parish or congregation, and for the Cradle Catholics in your community.

See where the Spirit leads you as your understanding of the teachings and commands of Jesus increases, you develop a deep sense of peace, and a joy for life.

Based on my own experience, I've started sketching out the sequel to this book. The goal of the sequel is to take you from experiencing the peace of someone who has been reborn onto the path of discipleship, growing even closer to God. The sequel book will likely include sections exploring:

- **Love One Another** – Jesus' command to "love one another as I have loved you", the "mutuality commands" that echo throughout the New Testament. Love is another core pattern of Jesus.

- **The Holy Spirit** – Cradle Catholics talk about the Holy Spirit but how many experience the Holy Spirit and are led by the Spirit?

- **Understanding God's Will** – If as a disciple you are working to serve God, wouldn't it be helpful to know what God's goals and objectives are? Wouldn't it be helpful to know specifically how you can ask Him for help in working to achieve His goals and objectives?

- **Praying Effectively** – If you understand the purpose of prayer, and if you take the time to understand God's goals and objectives, you'll probably pray very differently that you're praying now.

That's a sketch of where the next book is now.

peace be with *you*.

<fine dell'inizio>

LIST OF ACTIVITIES

Activity 1.1: God's Grace in My Own Words

Activity 1.2: Amazing Grace Musical Study

Activity 1.3: Paul & Peter's Use of the Word "Grace" Study

Activity 1.4: Accepting God's Gift of Grace

Activity 2.1: List of Unforgiven People

Activity 2.2: Immediate Forgiveness Exercise

Activity 3.1: Rate Your Current Level of Bible Reading & Study

Activity 3.2: Jesus' Instructions for Living

Activity 3.3: Gospel of Mark DVD Reflection & Notes

Activity 3.4: Gospel of John DVD Reflection & Notes

Activity 3.5: The "Other 42% of the Good News" Study (Group Activity)

Activity 4.1: Rate Your Current Level of Peace

Activity 4.2: Identify People at Peace

Activity 4.3: Freedom from Fear Study & Pledge

Activity 4.4: Freedom from Worry Study & Pledge

Activity 4.5: Feet Washing Plan

Activity 4.6: Sermon on the Mount Top 3 List

* * *

50297364R00087

Made in the USA
Charleston, SC
20 December 2015